LIBERATION,
THE JESUS MODE

LIBERATION, THE JESUS MODE

Reflections on the Gospel for the B–cycle

Joseph G. Donders

ORBIS BOOKS

Maryknoll, New York 10545

The Catholic Foreign Mission Society of America (Maryknoll) recruits and trains people for overseas missionary service. Through Orbis Books Maryknoll aims to foster the international dialogue that is essential to mission. The books published, however, reflect the opinions of their authors and are not meant to represent the official position of the society.

Copyright © 1987 by Joseph G. Donders
All rights reserved
Published in the United States of America by Orbis Books, Maryknoll, N.Y. 10545
Manufactured in the United States of America

Manuscript editor: Lisa McGaw

Library of Congress Cataloging-in-Publication Data

Donders, Joseph G.
  Jesus, the liberation mode.

  Includes index.
    1. Bible. N.T. Gospels—Meditations.   I. Title.
BS2555.4.D67 1987   242′.3   87-5700
ISBN 0-88344-553-0

This tenth book in the series of Reflections on the Gospels, published by Orbis Books, is dedicated to Philip Scharper, for so many years the Editor-in-Chief of Orbis Books. It was only some days before his terminal illness that he was asked if he would allow the dedication of this book to him. He very graciously accepted this dedication. At that moment nobody knew that the author would be invited to give a commemorative eulogy some weeks later in Saint Patrick's Cathedral in New York. We thought it fitting to begin this book with that reflection on Philip Scharper, the person who helped so many to see Jesus Christ as a Liberator.

We come together
to commemorate our friend Philip Scharper.
The fact that we do this
is an indication
that he
is important to us,
that his life is relevant
and significant
to our lives.
Why?

There are most probably as many answers
to that question
as there are people here,
as there are people
who know him.
Yet, hearing about him,
reading about him,
and talking about him,
one thing seems to have struck
everyone:
the way he cherished and fostered
the wideness of his mind and his heart.
To say it
in a term left to us
by the one
so many of us choose
to interpret,
to understand,
to explain,
and to guide
our lives,
Jesus of Nazareth:
Philip Scharper
was a good shepherd
to his flock.
You know
from your own personal experience,
how you are all created
as a center of the universe.
We are created relating to all the rest,
we are created hanging together,
we are created taken up in a history,
we are created all-included and all-including,
containing the ends of the world.
It is in this, our universe,
that Jesus from Nazareth
asked each one of us
to be a good shepherd
to that reality
of ourselves

    after having given
    an example of this attitude,
    of this lifestyle
    to all of us.
Philip Scharper was a good shepherd
to his universe,
he was a good shepherd
to his flock.
He took care of all of them
by his interest
in the nearby and the far-off,
in those from South America,
and those from Europe,
in those from Asia,
and those from Africa,
in the poor and the rich,
being in charge of that publishing house
Orbis,
the world,
the universe.

    It is not only
    by all his editing
    and publishing,
    by his interviewing
    and listening
    that he
    —in the most literal sense—
    changed
    his and our world,
    he did that also
    by living
    his type of life.
One of the difficulties in our days
is
that our old spiritualities,
that the old ways in which we lived,
that our former Christian lives
do not seem to correspond
to our new experiences
anymore.

Don't we find
in a life
as lived by Philip Scharper
a model
as wide as the world,
as wide as the universe,
with that special interest in the nearby
that is the guarantee
that the far-off
does not turn into a mere abstraction?
Didn't he live
as wide and loving
a life
as our lives should be?
When at the end of his life
Jesus met his friends
for one of the last times,
he asked them:
"Do you love me?"
and when they answered
"Yes!"
he added:
"If you do,
take care of my sheep,
take care of your universe,
be a good shepherd,
a good friend to all,
to your whole universe!"
The work done
by Philip Scharper,
everything he left behind,
the life he lived,
is worthy to be commemorated,
not only in view of him
but because of us,
who are left behind.

CONTENTS

INTRODUCTION

Jesus came to redeem
us.
Jesus came to liberate
us.
He did not come to liberate
God.
    He did not come
    to free
    either God,
    or us,
    from God's wrath,
    though very many think
    and thought so,
    and though our catechisms
    are full of that.
    God did not need anyone
    or anything
    to be free
    to want
    and to love us.
He came to liberate us
from those
who do not want us to be
the divine creatures
we are,
he came to free us
from those
who do not want us to know
the immense potentialities
we have;

1

he came to free us
from those
who tell us
that we are only
poor and miserable,
sinners and stupid,
restricted and limited,
relative and small,
ourselves included.

    Did you never notice
    how those in charge
    do not want us to know,
    did you never see
    how those in power
    do not want us to be informed,
    did you never notice
    how doctors and lawyers,
    how merchants and farmers,
    how industrialists and managers,
    how teachers and professors,
    how politicians and journalists,
    how generals and police commanders,
    how priests, bishops, and popes
    always seem
    to try to hide
    the truth
    from us,
    keeping us ignorant
    on purpose?
    And we are to blame,
    because we let them
    do that,
    doing the same.
He came to tell us,
he came to show us,
who we are,
and what we can do,
how God's own light
and God's warmth,

how God's love
and God's life
are in the mind
and heart
of every one
of us,
his followers,
the old and the young,
women and men,
disabled and abled,
the northern,
the western,
the southern
and the eastern.
  He did not come only
  to liberate you,
  yourself,
  of all diminishment,
  frustration,
  and sin;
  he did not come only
  to show you
  who you can be,
      he came to ask you,
      he came to invite you,
      he came to entice you,
      he came to convince you,
      he came to implore you,
      he came to plead with you,
      to be a liberator
      of all the others,
      as he was and is,
      because we,
      too,
      like so many
      around us,
      are tempted
      to keep others
      ignorant and small,

        stupid
        and *in their place*,
        in order to glory
        and profit.
Aren't we the doctors and the lawyers,
the merchants and the farmers,
the industrialists and the managers,
the teachers and the professors,
the politicians and the journalists,
the generals and the police commanders,
the priests, the bishops, and the popes,
in our world?
        He,
        that glorious Jesus,
        showed us
        how to be,
        revealing to us
        the power,
        and the freedom,
        of the children of God.
Let it be,
oh,
let it be!

1.

TWO THOUSAND YEARS LATER

Mark 13:33–37

He was born almost two thousand years ago.
All the time before,
people had been hoping for him,
in each sigh,
at each misunderstanding,
before each fight,
after each departure,
at each death,
all that time,
all the time. . . .
      Each child hanging its empty stocking
      or putting its empty shoe
      under the chimney,
      —even if the flue
      is not really there
      anymore—
      before Christmas,
      is still an expression
      a symbol,

a sign,
of the everlasting hope
that gifts will come down,
from above,
from the sky,
and that all desires,
all hopes,
and all wishes
will be fulfilled,
though it might mean
to that child
getting a Cabbage-Patch doll
or a robot man only.
Christ was born
two thousand years ago,
but humanity's desires
have not yet been fulfilled.
There are one hundred fifty million starving people
in Africa,
the continent
he knew so well as a refugee,
who are looking to the sky each day,
hoping for some relief,
some beans,
some corn,
and some oil.
Christ was born
two thousand years ago,
but for many it is as if
nothing happened that night.
In a town like Chicago,
two hundred fifty thousand human beings
will sleep in the streets,
looking for some shelter,
as his parents did
before he was born.
Christ was born
two thousand years ago,
but there is less peace in the air
than when the angels sang that night:

the sky being full
of warplanes and satellites
that form a threat,
not only to the newly born babes
in Bethlehem,
but to all of us.
    He is obviously away,
    like the man
    in the Gospel of today,
    who left for a far-off country,
    a man traveling abroad.
He had been speaking
about returning to his Father,
that is true,
but hadn't he
—before he left—
assigned them their tasks;
hadn't he entrusted his home,
this world,
to those
who followed him,
to those
who seemed to have understood
that they had been equipped,
as he was:
    to fulfill all desires,
    to heal all wounds,
    to bring all together
    round one table?
And hadn't he told
them,
and us,
that he would be back soon,
hoping to find us
not *asleep?*
    Isn't that
    what we are:
    asleep in a world
    that needs
    to wake up?

That is why,
again,
we should prepare
for him.

2.

ARE YOU GOING?

Mark 1:1–8

When the people around him
heard of John the Baptizer,
they were facing a problem.
Were they going
to hear him,
or were they going
to stay at home?
The problem must have divided many a family:
the daughter was going,
the son remained home;
mother wanted to go
but father said:
"You are not going,
you stay home,
and I am not going either!"
     There is hardly a description
     of who went,
     though we know
     that there were some tax collectors,
     and some soldiers,
     who asked him:

"Listen,
what should we do?"
Why did some go,
and why did others stay home?
We can only guess.
We can guess,
because we could ask ourselves too:
would I have gone,
or would I have stayed home?
Would we go to a man like John?

Would you go,
if you heard
that a kind of tramp,
straight out of the mountains,
had started to preach
conversion,
a change of the world,
and a change of yourself
in a river nearby?
I think that very many of us
would not go at all,
and that we might even forbid our children
to go there,
too.
We know that his world
is not all that good,
we know, maybe, that we should change,
but I wonder
whether we would be willing
to go to John.

Too many of us
are like that man,
who has a pain in his stomach,
a very serious pain,
he does not only feel some butterflies
in that stomach;
it is as if
he feels a fire in it.

He should go and see the doctor,
everyone says,
but he does not.
He does not,
because,
though he would like to know
what is wrong with him
and his stomach,
he is at the same time afraid
of the truth.
He is also afraid
of something else.
He likes meat very much,
He is a real carnivore,
and it is not the meat he likes
so very much,
but the fat,
the grease
that comes with meat.
He simply loves
those yellow strips
of greasy fat.
He loves
everything
that is greasy and fat,
he would not even mind
to drink all the gravy,
if he could.
Sometimes
he does.
He does not go
to that doctor,
because he is afraid
that the doctor will tell the truth
about his health,
and that he would hear
that he has to change
his diet:

no oil,
no fat,
no grease,
no gravy
at all.
It was
for a such-like reason,
that many did not go
to John the Baptist.
They were afraid,
that he would tell them
the truth,
and that they would be told
to change their lives.

    I am afraid
    that for that very same reason,
    many of us
    would not go either,
    being afraid,
    too!

We are willing
to celebrate Christmas,
oh yes!
We can't even wait,
all decorations are up
in our streets and in our homes
from the beginning of Advent.
But who wants to prepare
for Christmas
by listening to John,
and the Christmas hopes
he expresses
in the name of God,
asking us to change
our style of life?

    Would you have gone
    to listen to John,
    that prophet at the riverside?

Would you go now,
if you heard
that he returned there?
Would you go?

3.

HOPE WE NEED

John 1:6–8, 19–28

Isaiah says:
"Listen,
justice shall be done."
Paul writes:
"Christ will come."
John preaches:
"He is already among you."
All three want to give us
hope.
>You might say,
>what is hope?
>Hope does not help.
>You can't buy anything
>with hope.
>Hope is nice,
>but it is so thin.
>It means only
>that you don't have the thing
>you would like to get.
Hope
is very important,

and we know
that well.
    There is someone
    seriously ill.
    You love her very much.
    She is so sick
    that she was taken to a hospital.
    The doctors say
    that she might come through,
    if her attitude
    would be positive,
    that is to say,
    if she would desire
    and hope
    to live.
Every time you visit her,
she turns her face
away from you
when you enter her room,
and she says:
"Don't bother,
get away,
leave me alone,
it is too late,
it is finished,
I am finished
you better start
forgetting about me,
this is the end,
I feel it."
    You speak about things
    you would like to do
    with her,
        a party,
        a dinner,
        a visit,
        a trip overseas,
        even a pilgrimage,

    but there is no interest,
    no reaction
    at all.
And the doctors say:
"We are afraid
that she will be slipping away from us,
there does not seem to be
any will to live in her,
no hope."
    Every day she is weaker,
    and thinner,
    and paler.
    She really will escape
    from you,
    and from the world,
    if she does not pick up her spirit,
    and hope to live.
    Without that will from within,
    operations,
    chemicals,
    radiations,
    surgery,
    pills,
    powders,
    injections,
    and pep talks
    will be to no avail
    at all.
    She will linger
    and die.
It is in this way
that we need hope,
in our world,
and in our lives.
    I am not going to give you
    a long list
    of all the things that are wrong
    in our own lives
    and in the lives of so many others.

Think of the starving in Africa,
the homeless in the American towns,
the prisoners in so many countries,
the neglected youth all over the world,
the difficulties in your own family,
around your very own kitchen table.
Even without a full list
we know that we are sick,
that we suffer many ailments.
John preaches:
"It will change!"
Paul writes:
"He is faithful!"
Isaiah says:
"Justice will reign!"
We should hope so.
We should believe it.
And all that hope and belief
will make us pick up our spirits
and do from
within ourselves
whatever we can
to heal,
to survive,
and to be thankful
for life regained
in that birth
we are going to celebrate
at Christmas.
Amen.

12/19/87

4.

GIVING BIRTH TO GOD

Luke 1:26–38

It is almost Christmas,
only a few days to go.
Today the Gospel tells us
how it all started in Mary:
     How an angel came down,
     how light spread over her,
     how a cloud descended,
     how she looked up
     from whatever she was doing,
     and how Gabriel asked her
     to participate in God's plan
     by giving birth to Jesus.
No explanations
on what she could expect;
no long lessons
on what it all entailed;
no quick survey
of all prophecies
from Genesis to Malachi,
nothing of the kind.

18

It was as if Mary
had been waiting for it,
as if she had been informed,
as if she had been initiated in all this
long before.
She only never had thought
that she would be the one.
That must have been the reason
that she was amazed.
That is why
it did not start for Mary
that day.
It had started long before,
while she was working,
while she was praying,
while she was hoping
that one day
her people,
and all peoples,
would be liberated
and redeemed.

You might even say,
that what was born from her
had been conceived by her
even long before Jesus' conception
in her womb.
Working,
praying,
hoping,
she in her very simple way
had been *birthing*
God,
and God's goodness
long before.

Long, very long ago,
more then six hundred years ago
there lived a Dominican mystic
among the Celts in Europe
Meister Eckhart of Hochheim (ca. 1260–1327).

He said something very strange,
something that never got lost
during all those centuries.
He wrote:
"What good is it to me
if Mary gave birth to the Son of God
fourteen hundred years ago,
and I do not also give birth to the Son of God
in my time and in my culture."
That is why I told you
that Mary had been birthing
God,
and God's goodness,
long before she conceived Jesus.

She birthed God
during her pregnancy,
she did it when giving birth to Jesus;
she had done it before,
and she remained doing it afterward.
That is what we should do
giving birth to God
and God's goodness in us
in the world in which we live.
Amen.

12/25

5.

CHRISTMAS PRESENTS AND CHRISTMAS LIGHTS

Luke 2:1–14

We often use symbols
that have lost their meaning;
signs,
without an obvious sense.
Somewhere in the north of Holland
there is a church,
where all those who entered
used to bow down
in the direction of a whitewashed part
of the church wall
before settling in the pews.
Nobody knew why.
One had been doing this
from generation to generation,
and in fact
no question was ever asked.
 Then, one day,
 the parish council
 decided to clean the walls.

While doing this
one discovered some traces of a painting
under the whitewash on the wall,
Very carefully one started to peel off the chalk,
and one uncovered
a centuries-old painting of Jesus
on the cross.
Nobody remembered that picture,
there was no description to be found,
the painting was lost
from human memory.
It must have been painted over
centuries before.
But the sign of respect
had remained,
one finally knew
why one was bowing one's head
before sitting down.
The sign had been there,
its meaning was forgotten.
Nobody knew the story
of the origin of that sign,
nobody could tell its tale.

    Driving through the towns and villages
    during this Christmas night,
    one sees everywhere
    lights red,
        orange,
        green,
        yellow,
        blue, and
        pink.
    Driving like that,
    you will be driving alone,
    because everyone is at home,
    giving presents and gifts
    to each other,
    millions of them.

Those lights
brightening up the darkness of our world,
those gifts
fulfilling so many wishes and desires,
are obviously signs and symbols, too.
But who would understand them
if the Christmas story
is not remembered
and told?

    The story about
    how they had been looking for him
    all through the ages.
    How even today
    so many are hoping for a redeemer.
    And how finally
    he came from God,
    God's gift to the world,
    a light
    brightening its darkness.

You should tell this story
to yourself:
how in your own world
that often seems so frustrating
and lonely,
new life was born.

    You should tell it
    to those around you,
    to give them the hope
    they need so very much.

But you should especially tell it
to your children,
just as your parents
told you
the Christmas story.

    It is the nicest story in the world,
    if you come to think of it:
    how God started a new life
    in our midst.

It is in this way
that we can recapture
the meaning of the lights
we light in the night,
of the gifts
we give each other
fulfilling our desires.
    That is why we came here together
    in the middle of the night
    starting the new life
    he gave us.

1/3/87

6.

A PROBLEM FAMILY

Luke 2:22–40

Long,
long ago,
when I was studying to be a priest
we were taught
how to preach.
We got assignments,
and my first assignment was
to make a sermon on the feast of today,
the Holy Family.
It was the very first sermon
I ever made.
I gave the sermon
to my professor,
and some of my fellow students.
I got a rather high mark,
and I was so proud of my first homily
that I sent a copy
to my father and my mother
at home,
to ask them
what they thought of it.

After a fortnight or so
my father,
father of nine sons and four daughters,
wrote me a letter,
something he very rarely did.
He wrote that he was impressed,
but that he did not like my sermon,
because,
he added,
it was neither to him,
nor to my mother,
and the rest of the family,
of any help at all.
He explained to me
why he thought so.
He said that the Holy Family
in my description was as unrealistic
as the figures in a Christmas group,
where mother Mary
kneels immediately after having given birth,
sitting on her knees next to the child,
when in her condition
she should be lying on a bed;
and where Joseph,
with a vaguely wondering smile,
and slightly out of place,
was standing
with a useless stick in his hands
at the other side of the manger,
while he could have been doing
more useful things.
My father was right,
and later I heard and read
too often
sugary and over-pious sermons
on the Holy Family,
not only from young priests,
but even from older ones,
bishops and popes included.

That Holy Family
was not an easy one,
and not a smooth one either,
It was a problem family,
with terrible misunderstandings
and conflicts.
That is why
it might be such a good example
for most of our own families,
or what is left of them.
        Are you surprised?
        Don't you remember,
        how Mary became pregnant,
        without Joseph knowing of anything?
        Don't you remember,
        how Joseph was already packing,
        ready to drop her,
        when the angel came,
        who changed his mind?
Did you forget
about their trouble in Bethlehem,
all those angels,
and shepherds,
and wise men,
with their stories,
even Mary did not understand?
Doesn't the Gospel reading of today indicate
how poorly off they were,
not being able to sacrifice
the normal offering of a lamb
at the occasion of the circumcision of their son,
but only the gift of the poor,
some little birds?
Did you not hear just now,
how Simeon gladly announced
that a sword would pierce the heart
of the mother?
        Don't you remember
        their flight to Egypt,

in the middle of the night,
with the cries of the murdered children in Bethlehem
haunting them?
Don't you remember
how he ran away from them,
and how they had to look for three days,
before they found him
in the temple.
Don't you remember,
how his mother told him off,
asking him:
"For heaven's sake,
how could you do
a thing like that
to us?"
and how he had answered:
"Indeed,
for heaven's sake"?
Did you forget
that the difficulties
and the misunderstandings
did not even stop
when he had grown up?
Don't you remember
how Mary and the rest of the family,
hearing about his preaching
and his miracles
got scared,
and how they came after him,
to get him back home,
thinking that he had lost his mind?
Don't you remember
that even at that marriage at Cana,
they did not seem to have understood each other
too well?
It was not an easy family,
not even a very normal family,
but in one thing they excelled,
and that is where they should be
our model and example:

they remained faithful to each other
whatever happened to them,
faithful till the end.

Most probably Mary did not understand
very much of her son
until after Pentecost,
but when she heard about his arrest,
his torture and his condemnation,
she came over to Jerusalem
to be with her son,
notwithstanding the enormous pain
and cost to her mother's heart.
She was standing there,
while he was bleeding to death,
faithful like a rock,
and he remained faithful to her,
even then,
for some of his last words
were for her,
when he told John,
standing there also:
"John, when you go home tonight,
take care of my mother!"
and John must have said:
"Yes, I will!"

Wives give life to their husbands,
husbands give life to their wives,
parents give life to their chidren,
children give life to their parents,
making them fathers and mothers.
All of them
should be faithful to that life,
whatever else might divide them,
just as God is always faithful
to the life God gave us.

To conclude practically:
if you remember
that you did not ~~contact~~ *open your heart + mind*
your husband and your wife,
your father or your mother,

your son or your daughter,
over the last Christmas season,
because of some bitterness ~~or preoccupation~~
between the two of you, or concern with your own self
please ~~contact her,~~ share with her,
please ~~contact him,~~ share with him,
today
because of the new year
that is so near,
but mainly
to be faithful to each other
as they were
in that Holy Family in Nazareth.

1/6/88

7.

THAT MULTICOLORED STAR

Matthew 2:1–12

One evening that star arose,
in the east.
Everyone could see it,
a star is a public thing.
It is very difficult to describe
the colors of a star,
especially if you remain looking at it:
it has all kinds of colors.
A star is like a diamond.
Who can describe the colors of a diamond?
    You turn it like this,
    and it is blue,
    bluer than the bluest sky.
    You turn it like that
    and it is red,
    redder than the reddest blood.
    You look at it
    from this side,
    and it is green,
    greener than the greenest grass.

You look at it from the other side,
and it is orange,
more orange than any orange
you ever saw before.
It is the same with a human person.
It is very difficult to describe a human person.
Once someone I knew very well died.
I was asked to say something about him.
So I went to several people who had known him,
and I was amazed.
One said:
"I loved him very much,
he was the most lovable person
I ever met in my life."
Another one said:
"I hate to say it,
as he is dead,
but I loathed that man,
I never liked him at all."
One said:
"He was so optimistic
and so full of pep";
another said:
"He was so dark-mooded,
and so lazy."

I started to realize
that it was very difficult to find out
who my friend really was,
they all looked at him
from their own point of view.
It is even more difficult to describe God.
Humanity does that in all kinds of ways.
The Jews did not even pronounce his name.
The Christians call God *Father,*
and they start calling God *Mother* now, too.
The Muslims say *Allah.*
The Africans have hundreds of names
like *The Discerner of Hearts,*
because God sees both the inside and the outside of a person;

The Great Eye,
because God sees all;
The Sun,
because God's light is everywhere,
or *The One who Clears the Forest,*
because God keeps the power
of the plants and the animals in the jungle under control.
And secularized people often speak about God,
as about the One who does not exist.

It is unbelievable,
and yet, they are all speaking
about the same reality.
They all do it differently,
and maybe not so differently.
Think of that diamond.
Who is right,
the one who says:
blue,
the one who says:
red,
the one who says:
green,
or the one who says:
orange?
Aren't they all right;
shouldn't all those colors
be seen together,
don't they complement
each other?
Today we celebrate Epiphany,
we commemorate how Jesus appeared to the nations.
He was born in Bethlehem,
the old Jewish royal town of David.
He was born from Jewish stock,
a real Jew.
That is why his parents
dedicated him last week
in the temple
to Yahweh.

Did that mean
that he had come only for the Jews?
Did that mean
that he is going to limit himself
to them?
The answer is given today,
the answer is clear:
no.
The people who arrived in Bethlehem
today
are non-Jews.
They are even different from each other.
When you look at them there
in the Christmas group,
you can easily see that:
one is black,
one is yellow,
and one is white.
They did not come only with different gifts,
gold,
frankincense,
and myrrh;
they came also with different personalities,
with a different history,
from different countries,
with different cultures.
And that little child Jesus,
our universal brother,
received them all,
with a very broad smile
on his lovely face!
Sometimes we think
that we are the chosen ones,
that we are the only ones,
that we know it all,
and that neither human,
nor God,
would be able to add
anything of value to us.

We should learn today,
that we should be open,
like Jesus
in that manger in Bethlehem,
open to all,
without drawing lines
between them and us,
without making any difference
between color and race,
without any discrimination
at all.

1/10/88

8.

THE CHOICE HE MADE

Mark 1:7–11

Some time ago
a very famous Norwegian actress
Liv Ullmann
was interviewed on television.
She was interviewed
because she had just written a book,
a kind of autobiography,
a book about herself,
entitled *Choices.*
    She told
    how she had become an actress,
    how she loved her success
    at home and on Broadway,
    in the theater plays,
    and on the screen;
    but that very often,
    while she was standing in the wings of the stage,
    made up as someone else,
    dressed as someone else,
    speaking someone else's words,

she wondered
whether she should not be herself,
unfolding herself,
instead of being always someone else.
One day she made the choice to do so,
she changed her life,
and started to be interested in others,
she became a kind of roaming envoy,
visiting the poor and forgotten
in our world.

I think that we might say,
that we celebrate today,
that something like this
happened to Jesus
in Nazareth.
He had been living in Nazareth
for very long,
he had been kind,
he had been very good,
he had always been doing
what people expected,
but then,
one day,
after about thirty years,
he decided to change,
to make another choice,
to unfold himself
further.

One night he went to bed,
knowing that next day,
he would leave the town.
It was the last time
that he slept on his own bed.
Did he tell his mother?
I don't know.
Did he write her a letter,
she found on his bed next morning?
I don't know that either.

One thing I do know:
he left,
and he went to John the Baptizer.
And while he was baptized,
in order
to unfold more and better,
from *within,*
heaven split open,
God came down,
in the form of bird,
the symbol of life and freedom,
and a voice spoke
and said:
"This is my Son"
    —or to translate
    that voice
    in another way—
"That's my boy!"
    That actress and film star
    Liv Ullmann
    did not only answer questions
    during that interview,
    she asked some questions.
    She asked her interviewer:
        "Do you watch television?
        Do you ever go to a film,
        and if you do,
        did you see any film,
        or any show
        over the last year,
        that helped you
        to discover who you are,
        that helped you
        to see what is in you,
        and to unfold your own riches,
        and your inner life?
        Was it not all about war,
        and spaceships,
        and things like that?"

Today we celebrate
how Jesus made the decision
to open himself,
to unfold God's life
in him;
we should do the same,
we should live the riches
we received.
We should do
what he did.
We should do
the very same.

  And above you,
  too,
  heaven will break,
  and a bird will fly up,
  indicating how you,
  too,
  are born to greater things.

1/17/88

9.

HIS GLORY AT HOME

John 1:35–42

The readings today
begin with the story
of a boy of twelve.
God called him
three times,
but he did not recognize
God's voice,
because,
as the reading reads:
> "He was not yet familiar with the Lord,
> because the Lord had not revealed
> anything to him as yet."

How many of us
are inclined
to think about
ourselves like that?
How many of us
are inclined
to say that we never heard
the voice of God?

Wouldn't the difficulty be
that we did not recognize
God's voice
when God spoke?
>   John the Baptizer
>   had recognized that voice,
>   from his very youth.
>   He had recognized that voice
>   when he left his home,
>   very early in his life.
Now Jesus had chosen
to leave that home,
to be more involved,
to unfold himself further.
He had chosen
to leave that home,
to be discovered,
to show God
alive in our world.
>   John
>   had seen him coming
>   from afar,
>   and as soon
>   as he was sure
>   it was Jesus,
>   he told his disciples
>   what he knew,
>   but what they
>   could not have discovered as yet:
> >   "Look,
> >   there is the Lamb of God!"
Two of John's disciples
decided
to follow him:
Andrew,
the brother of Peter,
and the one
who wrote the report of today:
John.

It was four o'clock
in the afternoon,
when they met;
an hour never
to forget.
       They started to walk
       behind him,
       they started to follow
       him
       on his heels.
       Something nobody likes,
Jesus did not either.
He turned around,
as we would have done,
and he asked them:
       "What
       are you looking for?"
They answered:
       "Teacher,
       where do you stay?"
And he said:
       "Come,
       and see."
There was no hesitation.
They were welcome at his home.
They were allowed in his kitchen,
he had nothing to hide.
They saw what he ate,
they saw what he drank,
they heard his words,
they noticed
how he related to others,
they saw his family,
they saw his friends,
and they liked all of it.
They stayed with him
that evening,
and maybe they even stayed with him
that night,

but whatever time
they spent with him
in that house in Bethany,
they saw
what John had seen.
They saw salvation,
            redemption,
            liberation,
            and celebration;
they saw God
in him.
        We know that
        because
        the next day
        Andrew looked for
        his brother Simon
            —later the Rock—
        to tell him,
        that they had found
        the Savior of the World,
        the Messiah.
There is not a word on a miracle,
no evil spirits were chased away,
no resurrections,
no transfigurations,
just they
and he
at home.
        They ate,
        they drank,
        they talked,
        they made an evening stroll,
        there were some visitors,
        the ordinary life at home,
        but through all that
        it became clear to them
        that in this friend
        they had met
        divinity was found,

just as John the Baptizer
had said.
They did not believe it
anymore
because their master had told them;
they believed it
because they themselves had seen.
They found it
in the life
he was living
at his home.
They found God
at home,
as we should,
and as we do
        —I am sure—
now and then.
Isn't God
in the comforting word,
that is spoken to you,
or you speak
to someone else?
Don't you see God's greatness,
in your three-week-old grandchild
splashing
in her bathing tub?
Aren't you tasting
God's care,
in the nice hot soup
you eat
on a very cold day?
Wasn't the artist
who painted
that picture
you like so very much
on the wall in your living room
a real gift from God
to you?

And what about the care
God took,
to provide you with composers
to make for you the music
that exhilarates your heart?
Aren't we surrounded
by all kinds of signs
of God's goodness to us?
Isn't God
speaking
all the time
to us,
in our very homes?
They discovered
Jesus
while they were with him
at his home.
We can discover God,
when we are at home
with him,
in our home,
at our work,
anywhere.
And no one of us
should ever say:
"I am not familiar
with the Lord,
because the Lord has not revealed
anything to me as yet."
We shouldn't,
because it is simply
not true.
God has,
oh yes,
God has!

_1/24/88_

10.

ON BEING ALL WE ARE

Mark 1:14–20

It is the same story,
now reported
in another way,
to tell us
something different.
    At the beginning of the story
    he is alone,
    preaching
    the undoing of the past,
    asking
    to begin anew.
People had been following him,
they had been listening,
but no one
had made
any definite commitment
as yet.
    He had neither friends,
    nor enemies.
    It was all
    too new,

it was all
too fresh,
it was all
too green,
very many words,
and hardly
any facts.
It had come
too suddently,
too much:
too all-at-once.
He started to feel
the loneliness
facing his task.
He would have
to engage
the whole of the world.
He would have
to conspire together
all the Spirit
blown
in each one of them.
He would have
to build
the Body common to all.
It did not matter
where he would start.
It did not matter
because all
were called.
It did not matter
because all,
everyone around,
were carrying
the same Spark,
were hoping
with the same desire.
He looked
around himself,

while walking along the lake.
He saw some fishermen
casting out their nets;
he did not even know their names,
it was only later
that he learned
that they were called
Andrew and Simon;
he saw some other fishermen
hauling in their nets,
who later proved to be called
James and John.
    They reminded him,
    like anything else
        he saw,
        he heard,
        he touched,
        he smelled,
        he tasted,
    of the future
    to come,
    the kingdom of God,
    where all would be
    finally collected
    in the fullness
    of human life.
He saw
how they fished,
out of the dark of the lake
fish of all kinds,
    green and black,
    blue and pink,
    white and purple,
    large ones
    and small ones,
    fat ones
    and lean ones,
    round ones
    and flat ones;

and again he thought
of the oneness to come
in the variety found,
and he said:
    "Follow me,
    I will make you
    fishers of men!"
He met
fishermen.
He might have met
others
that day.
He would have called them,
too,
whoever they were,
whatever they might have been doing,
whatever profession
they exercised,
whatever qualification,
they had.
    It would not have made
    very much of a difference.
    He would have been able
    to see them all
    in that very same light,
    in that very same perspective,
    that made him see
    Andrew and Simon,
    James and John
    as fishers of men,
    in view of
    the future to come.
That is what he did,
later on:
    wife and husband,
    father and mother,
    sister and brother,
    friend and enemy,
    sinner and saint,

Jew and pagan,
accountant and physician,
scribe and Pharisee,
farmer and merchant,
cook and baker,
householder and tailor,
you and me
were all called
to follow him.
He would not have told us,
that he would make us
fishers of men,
that would have made no sense
to us at all,
except for those
who happen to fish;
but he would have seen us all,
in the way we are,
in the work we do,
  as possible participants
  in the process
  he saw at work
  in this world:
  the growing together
  of the human family,
  a reality,
  he used to like to call
  the kingdom of God.
He might have met you
that day;
he is meeting you
now,
saying:
  "You as you are,
  in whatever you do,
  follow me,
  build with me,
  grow with me,

so that
together
in Spirit and Body,
we may be
all we are."

1/31/88

11.

FREED FROM ALL EVIL THINGS

Mark 1:21–28

In the Gospel
of today,
Jesus chases
evil away.
Others would say,
he chased
a devil away.
    Whatever he did,
    one thing is clear,
    every time he did it,
    a human being was unbound,
    liberated,
    and freed
    from all kinds of limitations.
There was the girl
who had fits;
    there was the boy,
    who threw himself in the fire;
there was the man,
who ran around naked;

52

there was the woman
who could not stand up.
He touched them,
he prayed over them
he commanded them,
and whatever he did,
the fits were over,
the convulsions forgotten,
people were freed and liberated,
able to be themselves.
It is not necessary
to think of evil
as a person,
when hearing all this.
You might,
and there is nothing
against it,
but very often
the explanation seems
more simple,
and more understandable,
too.
When I was in Africa,
I knew a boy
who possessed
a very rare treasure
for a boy on that continent.
He had a bike,
a very old bike.
He was
very proud of it.
One day he brought it
to a bike shop
to have gears fitted to it.
When he came back for his bike,
the bike-shop owner told him
that the gears
that had been installed
cost eight hundred Kenyan shillings.

He did not have that money,
and he was threatened:
> "If you don't pay the money
> before the end of the month,
> I am going to sell your bike,
> to get out of my costs."
So he started to ask,
left,
right,
and center
for eight hundred shillings.
He asked me, too.
But I said,
what so many others had said
before me:
> "That old bike is not worth
> eight hundred shillings,
> forget about it."
He was desperate.
He was going to lose
the most precious thing
he had.
He could not sleep anymore,
he could not eat anymore.
> One day I came home,
> he was sitting
> in front of my house.
> When I entered I noticed immediately
> that something had happened.
> I don't know why.
> I looked around
> in the house
> and discovered
> that the radio had disappeared.
When I came outside,
he was still sitting there.
He asked me
whether there was anything wrong.

That question made me suspicious.
I took a risk,
and I told him:
>   "Listen, I know what you did.
>   Bring that radio back,
>   or I am going to call
>   the police."
He denied everything,
and he said:
>   "Don't think
>   that I am a thief.
>   I am no thief!"
I repeated:
>   "You heard
>   what I said."
A quarter of an hour later
he knocked at my door.
He asked me:
>   "Can you give me
>   three shillings?"
I asked him:
>   "What for?"
and he said:
>   "To get your radio."
He came back with the radio,
but when he gave it back to me,
he kept on repeating:
>   "Now, listen,
>   don't think I am a thief,
>   I am no thief!"
I looked at him, and said:
>   "All right,
>   you are no thief,
>   but who took
>   that radio?"
He looked away from me
and answered:
>   "The bike!"

I was amazed at first,
but then I started
to understand.
He was right,
that bike had become so important to him,
that it had taken him over completely,
he could think of nothing else,
he was possessed by his bike.
A thing
had mastered him.
A thing
had become
like an evil influence
in his life.
A thing
had robbed him of his freedom,
a thing
ruled him absolutely.

     Has not something like that
     happened to all of us?
     Aren't we sometimes lost
     to a thing,
     to a passion,
     that masters us completely,
     that robs us
     of our freedom and liberty?
It is from that evil
that Jesus came to deliver us,
it is from that evil
that he came to liberate us.

     And we should be like him
     toward others,
     and to ourselves,
     so that we all can
     grow and prosper,
     in the freedom
     of the children of God.

2/7/88

12.

HEALING AND THE KINGDOM

Mark 1:29–39

He had just started,
his heart and head
full of great ideals,
foreseeing and wanting
a total change of the world:
the introduction
of the kingdom of God;
but that morning it all threatened
to end up,
in some cups of coffee,
as it so often does.
      What happened?
      He came from the synagogue,
      a devil had been chased away.
      He went to the house of Simon Peter,
      most probably hoping for some breakfast,
      just as all of us would do.
      The lady of the house was sick,
      Simon's mother-in-law was in bed
      with fire in her bones,
      as the text reads,

a nice way to say
that she had a fever.
Jesus went up to her,
he took her hand,
and healed her.
She came out of her bed,
and started to wait on them,
in no time
they were sitting
in front of their breakfast.
Or,
translating this
in the realities of today,
in front of their cups of coffee.
In the meantime
the story spread
all through the place.
He was healing.
It remained,
however,
calm during the day;
nobody was allowed to move
as it was a sabbath,
but then in the evening
when walking was allowed,
they came from all sides,
they came in droves,
carrying,
pushing,
and pulling their sick;
young and old,
and he,
full of compassion,
healed as many
as he could handle
that evening.
Their enthusiasm grew,
at each blind one that saw,
at each crippled one that walked,

at each deaf one that heard,
at each possessed one that got free,
at each leg that was stretched
or lengthened.
    It got dark,
    the healed ones went home,
    and the sick ones,
    too,
    hoping for the day of tomorrow.
During the night,
he got restless,
he came from under his blanket,
he went outside,
he walked away from it all,
he disappeared into the desert,
and there he must have been asking himself:
    "Is this healing,
    are those cups of coffee,
    what I came to do?
    Is this my mission?
    Is it all?"
In the morning he knew
his answer.
    I think
    we all can understand
    what happened to him
    that night,
I think we do,
because all of us
have been in the same situation,
I am sure.
    Just remember:
    you had a friend,
    a friend with a problem,
    a very serious problem,
    maybe it was a drinking problem,
    and you said to yourself:
        "I have to do something about it,
        he or she is going to blazes,

you can't drink
the amount of bourbon
he is drinking;
you can't drink
the amount of sherry
she is drinking,
without serious harm.
I have to talk to him,
I have to talk to her."
First you delayed,
postponed,
and procrastinated,
but finally
you had sufficient courage,
to go to your friend to talk
and you sat down,
and you talked about the weather,
and you drank a cup of coffee,
and you talked about that coffee,
and again about the weather,
and about some other trivial things,
and when it got time to leave,
you had not spoken one word
about the mission
you had been on.

When the others discovered
that he had disappeared,
they went to look for him.
They needed him,
they thought,
because again
the sick were filling up
the yard in front of the house
where he had slept.
They asked him to come,
but he had made up his mind,
he had understood,
and he told them:

"No,
I have to move on,
I have to go on preaching
the kingdom of God,
because that is why I came!
Let us go!"
And they left.
What he made clear to them,
he wanted to make clear
to us.
We, too, often think
that he came only to heal,
to rid us
of a toothache,
a stomachache,
to save us from a danger,
or something like that.
He definitely did,
but that was not all;
he came to change
the whole world,
he came to introduce
the kingdom of God,
and that is more
than healing a sickness
or two.

When you look at television
on a Sunday morning,
with a cup of coffee in your hands,
your television screens are filled
with all kinds of healing,
blind see,
deaf hear,
livers and kidneys are restored,
legs are stretched and lengthened
in miraculous ways,
and even the dumb
suddenly start to speak.

If all that is
true and authentic,
   —and haven't you
   sometimes
   your doubts?—
it certainly belongs to
his kingdom,
but it is definitely not all.
That is what he understood
that night
in the desert
after his spate of healing.
   The kingdom of God
   is a complete overhaul,
   a totally new creation,
   that new world and humanity
   that the prophets
      —Jesus
      included—
   dreamed
   and spoke about.
Let us not drown the kingdom of God
in some cups of coffee,
let us not restrict it
to a sick tooth here,
or a sick stomach there.
Let us live
in the fullness
of its expectations:
   a new world,
   a new heaven,
   a new universe:
   God all in all.
   Amen.

2/14/88

13.

HIS COMPASSION

Mark 1:40–45

He walked away
from Capernaum.
He walked away
from the healing there.
He had explained to them
how he had come
for even more important things,
how he had come
in view of the kingdom of God,
in view of a new start to human life
here on earth,
and in all ages to come.
      He turned
      the first corner in the road
      on the way to that kingdom.
First
they did not see him coming,
he was on his knees
and he crept,
but then they saw him:

a leper,
hardly recognizable as a human being,
full of sores,
filthily dressed,
but addressing him:
    "If you do will so,
    you can cure me!"
Of course,
he could not refuse
when it came to it.
He was moved with pity.
The original word is stronger,
it says:
"his bowels turned over
with pity
at the sight of this man,
they turned into water,"
and not withstanding
all he had said before,
notwithstanding
his grandiose ideas and ideals
about the introduction of that kingdom,
about the change of the whole world,
about having no time to heal,
he went to him,
a thing he should not have done,
and even worse,
    —because that was absolutely forbidden
    by custom
    and law—
he *touched* him.
    The leper
    was no leper any longer.
Then he came to himself,
again,
and he must have thought:
    "My God,
    what did I do?"

because he said to the man:
    "Not a word
    to anyone!"
but how would you be able
to keep your mouth
shut
in a case like that?
    Hadn't he to explain
    what had happened to him
    to all those around?
    That is what he did,
    left, right, and center,
    up to the point
    that Jesus had to hide,
    wherever he went.
Yet,
whether he climbed
the highest mountaintop,
or penetrated
the deepest forest;
whether he tried to get lost
in the desert,
or sailed
to the middle of the sea,
they always were there,
waiting again and again,
to be healed
and to be blessed.
    Almost all commentators say
    that there is
    another version
    of this healing of the leper.
    In that version
    Jesus is not moved by pity,
    but by anger.
Why this anger?
Was he angry
because the man was sick?

Was he angry
because of the leper crossing his way?
Or was he angry
because of himself,
because of his compassion?
> I don't know.
> One thing is clear:
> he kept a balance
> between his desire
> to change
> the whole of the world
> and the concrete cases of misery
> in front of him.
His compassion was general
because it was particular;
it was particular
because it was so general.
> And we should be,
> no,
> we are
> like him.
It is difficult to realize
that we are like him,
in our days.
We seem to have lost his touch,
and his compassion.
Our hearts are hardened,
our bowels do not turn,
we have seen so much,
we have seen too much.
Every day we see dozens of people die
on our television screens,
we see them
sick and betrayed,
jilted and beaten up,
so often,
that we
hardly even notice anymore.

And even if we notice one
in the streets we pass,
on the corners we take,
why should we bend over them?
Isn't the government taking care,
with the taxes
we earned and paid?
Didn't we send considerable checks
to the many charitable funds
that exist only because of that?
Jesus kept a balance.
It seems
that it made him angry
that he had to do so,
but he did,
it was the only possible solution.
And so have we:
    helping in the concrete case
    we meet,
    whenever we can,
    and nevertheless
    not losing sight of our mission
    to take care
    that this whole world
    is going to change,
    changing in the kingdom
    he came to bring,
    a kingdom of justice and peace,
    an honorable place for all.
We should take that care,
determining our priorities,
investing our money,
formulating our prayers,
educating the young,
exercising our political rights,
guiding all
on the road toward
kingdom-to-come.

And at each corner
we will meet the leper
he met,
whether we like it
or not.
Just as
he did.

2/21/88

14.

THE GOOD NEWS

Mark 1:12–15

He must have been sitting down
very often
to consider the state of the nation.
He must have been worrying
very often
about the leadership around.
He must have been talking
very often
about the temple and its service.
He must have been doing all that
so often,
as he was like us
in all things
but sin.
    Doing it
    we compare
    the world in which we live
    with the vision
    of a world to come.
Speaking about injustice,
we know about justice.

Complaining about dishonesty,
we imply honesty.
Worrying about wars and violence,
we dream about peace.
Protesting discrimination and violence,
we suggest a more equitable world.
>We all do this,
>we are all
>charged with vision;
>we are all
>full of hope,
>but we don't come further,
>we don't move,
>we see
>as if blind,
>we hear
>as if deaf,
>we move
>as if paralyzed.
So did he,
up to the moment
that he entered that desert
for those forty long,
very long days.
>Full of Spirit,
>he was challenging his spirit;
>full of vision,
>he was facing his blindness;
>his ears ringing with the message,
>he was fighting his deafness;
>asked to move,
>he had to overcome his lameness.
Mark says
he was tempted,
shocked and shaken,
fighting with all that held him back,
struggling with everything
that kept him small,
restricted, paralyzed,

and fruitless,
fighting the devil-self.
>He was going to ask us
>to do the same;
>he was going to invite us,
>to follow him;
>he was going to show us,
>what we would be able to do.

But before turning to us,
before inviting others,
he fought and overcame himself
the indolence,
the immobility
he wants us to overcome.
>We can no longer
>just complain about the others,
>forgetting about ourselves.
>We can no longer
>think that the world will change,
>and our vision be fulfilled,
>without that we ourselves
>are changed
>and moved.

That is what he had learned
in the desert,
and that is why he came out of it
—changed himself—
to shout to us:
>"The time is ripe,
>the days are fulfilled,
>I overcame
>what holds you down,
>I could do it,
>you can do it,
>change
>and believe
>this good news."

2/28/88

SECOND SUNDAY OF LENT

15.

THE GLORY AWAITING US

Mark 9:2–10

Once on the mountaintop
he suddenly
started to change
before their wondering eyes.
He himself started to shine.
It was
as if he lost his substance,
but that was not really what he did,
because that shine,
    that light,
    and that radiance
remained so substantial,
that it dazzled them.
And it was not only
that he changed,
but all that belonged to him,
his dress,
his sandals,
all he was wearing,
too,
started to change,

to flow away,
and yet not flow away;
to stay,
and yet not stay.
     It was not only he himself
     and all he wore,
     that seemed to lose
     its contours,
     its forms,
     its shapes,
     its limitations,
     its borders;
     it was as if time
     stood still.
     No,
     time
     was not standing still
     either:
     it opened up,
     it lost its limits,
     its sequence,
     and countability,
     because they saw
          —clearer
          than the day,
          more brilliant
          than the sun—
     in the very same light
     that came out of him,
     others,
     others long dead,
     others long gone:
     Elijah appeared
     and Moses.
They were sure of that,
though afterward
they did not understand
how it all happened,
so soon,

so rapid,
so intense.
> Their *now*
> was taken up
> in *then*.
> Their *then*
> seemed to be totally
> *now*.

Simon said:
> —he hardly knew
> what to say,
> he hardly knew
> what he was saying—

Simon said:
> "Can't we remain here
> like this,
> we and you,
> Elijah and Moses,
> taken up in this light,
> taken up in this glory,
> can't this be
> our final state?"

Then a voice was heard,
it seemed to come from heaven
not from this earth,
from paradise itself,
creating the distance again,
they were accustomed to,
and all turned
normal again.
> Normal did not seem the right word,
> hadn't they seen
> that the normal is,
> maybe,
> that light and that shine,
> that glory and that power?

He stood in front of them,
as they had known him before,
fatigue in his eyes,

earth on his sandals,
and dust on his dress,
and he said:
> "Don't tell anyone,
> before you have seen me
> rise from the dead;
> before I have finished my work,
> before I have ended my course."

It was in that way
that he himself
remained separated
from his final moment of glory,
that day;
and that those disciples
remained separated from him,
and his glory,
too.
> Too much had still to be done,
> his course had not yet ended,
> his glory would not be revealed
> till the end.

He asked them to be quiet
until his glory would be revealed
after his struggle was over.
> That is what they did,
> knowing
> that they would be
> glorious with him
> —in their turn—
> after having fulfilled
> their mission
> in this world,
> just as we will.
> Amen.

3/6/88

16.

SPEAKING OF HIS BODY

John 2:13–25

He spoke of his body,
of the sanctuary
that was his body.
>   When we speak of our body,
>   we speak about it
>   from top to toe,
>   from the beginning
>   of our left middle finger
>   to the end
>   of our right middle finger,
>   we speak about something
>   that can be measured,
>   chemically analyzed,
>   and physically weighed.
It is rather clear
that that is not all
our body is.
We are breathing in and out
uninterruptedly;
we are processing outside materials,

proteins, vitamins, minerals, starches, fat,
continuously;
standing in the light
and the warmth of the stars
we are changing our color
endlessly;
we depend in our genetic recipes
on our parents and ancestors,
on what they did
and did not do,
on how they lived
and died;
we are influenced by others
constantly,
as I am now influenced by you
listening,
and you are now influenced by me
speaking.
>   We are in contact
>   with the whole of the world;
>   relating and related
>   to waters and trees,
>   to stars and seas,
>   to animals and flowers,
>   to the present and the past,
>   to the future and all the people
>   around,
>   and in a way
>   in us.
Most times
we don't notice it.
We are individualized,
we do not seem to need others,
sometimes we do not even want to need them,
very often we don't want to belong,
>   free from the world,
>   free from our fellow human beings,
>   free from God,

we play our Walkman,
and hurry off.
Others have a deeper insight
in that belonging;
people with what we sometimes call
a primal vision.
The Pygmies in the Zairean rain forest
who do not cut a tree
without a sacrifice of expiation.
Amerindians
in the American plains,
who did not kill an animal
without first asking its permission.
Those people
relate to the earth and the sky,
to each other,
and to God,
in a quite different way.
They know that they belong together,
that their only survival chance
is community,
forming one body
—so to speak—
with the world around.
In the Gospel today
Jesus speaks
about the sanctuary of his body.
He did that more often.
He experienced himself as connected
with everyone.
"I am the trunk,
you are the branches."
He saw himself
in *body* and *spirit*
related to everyone,
forming the one family of God.
He saw the whole of humanity,
the whole of creation,
as ONE PERSON;

and himself being PART
OF THAT ONE PERSON.
    We should have that vision,
    when we want to belong to him.
    We should have that vision,
    even when judging our world affairs.
I have been working very long in Africa,
in a context where we could do
a lot of serious research.
One of the questions
that intrigued us very much
was:
    Why do Africans want
    to become Christian?
Was it to be redeemed
from sin?
Yes
and No,
because they do not have
the Western idea of sin.
Was it to be saved
from hell?
Yes
and No,
because they had not a thing
like hell.
Why then?
    And the answer
    we almost always found
    was
    that they wanted
    a new life,
    that they wanted
    a larger community.
They understood
that they would not be able
to survive in our world
in their restricted,
traditional ethnic group.

They realized
that they had to join
the larger community
of the human family,
the family of God,
the body of Christ,
the body Jesus spoke about
in the Gospel of today.
>They understand this better than ever,
>now the full impact of Western culture
>is known
>and the disastrous effects
>of our recent policies
>—hunger and starvation—
>are in the open.

Today
Jesus speaks about
the sanctuary of his body,
how it would be saved,
how it would be collected together
in the end,
including all of us.
>Not only Africans are longing for that,
>Jesus was longing for it too,
>and so should we,
>in an effective,
>active
>way.

Amen.

17.

BACKED UP BY HIM

John 2:13–25

Being invited to speak about
the hunger and famine in Africa,
I have been giving lectures
all over the country.
While making that tour
here in the United States
I got, of course, some insight
into the situation here,
too.
> I spoke mainly to groups
> that were in one way or another
> trying to do something
> about the disastrous situation
> in Africa.
> But after the talk,
> after the questions,
> after the input,
> and the feedback,
> there was always
> that last question,
> that unavoidable question:

"Is there any hope?
Is humanity,
are we,
so sick,
that it would be
more realistic
just to give up?"
When that question was asked,
you could see people
quickly look at each other,
and at me,
checking the reactions,
and at the same time confirming
that this issue
had to be faced,
that this question
had to be answered.
The readings of today
are all three of them
on this very question.
The first reading
speaks about a situation
where all hope
seemed to be lost:
the people scattered
and disbanded:
vagrants only
on the wide face of this earth,
powerless,
sick,
and dying.
The second reading
explains how
we were,
or are,
dead through our sins,
because of our faulty options:
wrong decisions
and a poor list of priorities.

And in the third reading,
Jesus explains
that there was NO hope,
that he would be crucified,
lifted up on a cross,
and murdered.
 It is true,
 I think,
 that humanity is sick.
 It is true,
 I guess,
 that humanity
 might be called
 dying.
But it is also true
that in this world
another power is present:
the *power*
that brought us here together,
the *power*
that brings all the people
who are organizing themselves
in justice and peace groups
together,
again and again.
 When we think
 about Jesus' redeeming work,
 we often think
 about his blood shed,
 once and for all,
 about the pain suffered,
 so long ago,
 about the death endured
 on the cross.
 We have a vague impression
 that those events
 saved us.
In a way
that is true,

in another way,
it is not.
>What saved us,
>and what saves us,
>is that notwithstanding
>his suffering and death,
>the movement
>he had started in this world
>did not give up
>and never ended.

During his life
he had formed a small group
of hardly over ten people.
He had organized,
inspired,
and led them.
Together they had started
the struggle for a better world,
full of hope,
because they believed themselves
to be backed up
by him,
and by God.
>It is that group
>that did not disappear
>after his death,
>that remained existing,
>notwithstanding that death,
>and because of the Easter phenomenon
>we call
>resurrection.

A movement,
a process,
a growth,
a network,
that even reached us,
this very day,
and that is our hope
in this world.

If you,
effectively,
join that movement,
 that pattern,
 that network,
you will dispel
all gloom
and doom
together with him.

18.

HIS DEATH ON THE CROSS

John 3:14–21

The riddle is terrific,
the question enormous:
how is it
that there is so much suffering
in this world?
>It is the question
>that haunts those who are sick,
>those who are tortured or in prison,
>those who look at the suffering of a loved one,
>those who are hit by an accident,
>by cancer,
>by AIDS,
>by as common a thing as the flu,
>or a fever.
Aren't we wanted?
Were we a mistake?
Aren't we respected?
Aren't we loved?
>Sometimes the question is:
>"Why me?"
>Other times:
>"Why him, or her?"

Besides that suffering
there is the end of all suffering,
here on earth,
there is death.
Death
so radical
that the question:
"Why had I to die?"
was never asked
in this world,
except,
maybe,
by the ones Jesus raised
from the dead.

    Much suffering can be explained
    because of the reactions
    of our body system
    that wants to avoid
    death:
        my pain warns me
        that things are not well,
        it tells me
        to take care of myself,
        to change my lifestyle,
        to escape my environment,
        to be less involved,
        or less tense.
    Death is no warning,
    death is unavoidable,
    it will come for all of us,
    like a thief in the night,
    suddenly,
    or after a slow preparation:
    it will be there.

The house I built to live in,
will be inhabited by strangers.
The car I drove,
will be driven by others.
All the things so dear to me,
my clothing and my shoes,

my pipe and my watch,
my electronics and my souvenirs
will be thrown away,
without any pity,
neither for them
nor for me.
    Even if Jesus
    wouldn't have died on the cross,
    he would have had to die nevertheless,
    being in all things,
    except sin,
    equal to us.
It was this death,
much more than his suffering,
that posed the question:
Wasn't he wanted?
Was he a mistake?
Wasn't he respected?
Wasn't he loved?
He himself asked
that question:
    "Father,
    why did you
    forsake me?"
Others asked that question, too,
by saying:
    "Now we will see
    whether God loves you;
    ask to be saved
    from this cross,
    ask to be saved
    from death!"
        Are we all born for the abyss,
        for eternal darkness,
        like a sigh
        that starts and ends;
        like a feather that blows up
        in the wind,
        and falls;

     like an insect
     that flies around the fire,
     to be burnt;
     like an empty place in space;
     like a vain moment in time;
     like a blast of a trumpet
     that is heard,
     but then no longer?
Hanging on the cross,
he is dead
among us.
Looking at him,
we know
that he died.
There is no doubt about that.
Look at his mangled body,
     his crown of thorns,
     his drooping head,
     the blood all over,
     the nails in his feet and in his hands,
     the wound in his chest.
Yet, he is hanging there,
in our rooms,
and above our beds,
because we know
that his death was overcome,
that on that cross
death lost its sting,
that in him it was shown
that the grain has to die
to enter new,
eternal life.
     Do you remember
     how he was once seen
     transfigured and glorious
     in front of his disciples,
     shining,
     and shining,
     and shining . . . ?

What we see,
looking at him on the cross,
is only a fixed moment,
a "still"
in a process,
in which he acquired
the glory
prepared for him.

    Just so our suffering,
    and finally our death
    will only be moments,
    transitions,
    unbindings,
    and new relations
    in view of the light and the life
    that awaits those
    who live
    with the faith and the hope,
    he had
    and he has,
    he was
    and he is
    and who died
    in the light
    he brought,
    revealing the truth
    about us.

19.

GIVING LIFE

John 12:20–33

It is almost Easter,
Suddenly the shops
are full with
eggs:
> eggs in all sizes,
> eggs in all colors,
> eggs in all kinds of material,
> chocolate ones, and sugar ones,
> plastic ones and rubber ones,
> empty ones and full ones,
> red ones and purple ones,
> blue ones and white ones,
> real ones and man-made ones,
> cheap ones and very expensive ones.
Not only are those eggs in those shops,
very soon
they will also be
in the nests
birds will start building
in trees and in bushes,

91

that in their turn
are filled with the promise
of new life.
Everywhere
sticky brown and green buds
are waiting
to unfold
in the light
of the rising sun,
in the warmth
of the new day.
    Eggs
    and buds will burst open
    giving new life
    to God's glory
    in them.
The readings of this Sunday
are not about
that new life.
They are about
new life
in us.
The new life announced
in the reading from Jeremiah:
    "In those days,
    says the Lord,
    I will place my law
    within them,
    and write it
    upon their hearts.
    I will be their God,
    and they shall be my people,
    No longer
    will they have need
    to teach their friends and kinsmen,
    how to know the Lord.
    All from least to greatest
    shall know me,
    says the Lord."

We all
will be filled
with divine life.
    All this
    was totally true of Jesus,
    God's life among us,
    as a human being.
A life
that remained hidden
for very long.
    A life
    that burst out of its shell
    and started to bloom
    more and more
    the longer he lived.
A life
that found its fulfillment
when he died on the cross
and rose from that death
for us.
    A life
    that did not manifest itself
    without pain:
    old ways
    had to be left behind;
    the protective shell
    had to be broken;
    the bud
    had to get overstretched,
    and had to burst;
    the seed
    had to fall in the earth
    to die,
    giving way
    to God's glory.
Today he tells us
that we should be like him,
giving birth to the newness
already in us,

bringing to light
God's life
in us:
    God's compassion,
    God's goodness,
    God's relatedness,
    God's glory,
    God's love,
breaking through the shell,
that surrounded us
up to now too often
as a tomb,
while it should be
like a womb
from which God's life
is continually
born.
    While the whole of nature
    is preparing
    to show God's glory
    among us,
    we are commemorating
    how Jesus
    showed that glory
    too,
    inviting us to do
    the very same.
    Amen.

20.

THE JERUSALEM JOURNEY

Mark 11:1-10

It is today
that we commemorate
how he changed his direction,
how he started a new movement.
>   Up to then
>   he had been moving
>   into his own inner,
>   in the desert for forty days,
>   before that in Nazareth
>   for almost thirty years,
>   and even later so very often
>   during those nights
>   that he was on a mountaintop,
>   or hidden deep in the forest,
>   alone with himself,
>   alone with God
>   shining in his glory
>   from within.
Up to then
he had moved
from within that glorious center

in him
out to the others.
Coming out of the desert,
establishing himself
in the most cosmopolitan town
of his region,
  —or was he there
  just sleeping
  in a street,
  who knows?—
contacting
Jews and aliens,
Greeks and people from the Diaspora,
he had been traveling
in an ever wider circle,
as far as his feet
could carry him:
to Samaria and Bethany,
to the Decapolis,
and in the direction of Syria.
  He had met,
  and touched,
  all kinds of people:
    the woman from Samaria,
    the Roman officer,
    the Greeks looking for him,
    Nicodemus the Jewish scholar,
    Simon the Pharisee,
    and even the Syro-Phoenician lady,
    who asked his help.
Now he changed his direction.
He was not entering
into himself;
he was not going out
to others;
entering Jerusalem
he started that final movement
foretold by so many prophets,

the movement that would bring
all and everything
together.
      There were the animals,
      the ass and its colt;
      the branches,
      the leaves and the flowers,
      thrown under the feet
      of those animals;
      there were the sun and the sky;
      there were the stones
      and the cobbles in the street
      that threatened
      —according to
      his very own words—
to shout out
aloud;
there were the people,
the young and the old,
the rich and the poor,
full of expectation,
and yet not too sure
of what was going on,
pushing and pulling,
all around him,
singing and dancing,
shouting and ululating:
      "Glory to God,
      hail to the King,
      Son of God,
      Son of David,
      alleluia!"
There were also scribes,
friends and opponents,
who understood
better than anyone else,
what he started to do,
and where all this would lead to.

It was in their heads
that the old prophecies
tumbled and rumbled:
hadn't Zechariah prophesied,
that the Messiah would enter the town
sitting on the young of an ass? (Zech. 9:9)
Hadn't he spoken about a final day
when Yahweh would put his feet
on the Mount of Olives in Jerusalem? (Zech. 14:4)
Didn't Jesus act as a king,
when he simply sequestered
the animals he needed? (1 Sam. 8:17)
Didn't the book of Genesis tell
that the Messiah
would tie his young ass to the vine,
to its stock the foal of the she-ass? (Gen. 49:11)
And they were afraid,
not only for him,
but also of him.
And he,
sitting on his donkey,
surrounded
by the shouts and the colors,
the smells and the perfumes,
the excitement and the enthusiasm
of the people,
of this old Jerusalem,
he must have been thinking
of the new Jerusalem;
he must have been dreaming
about the great day
he foresaw,
when all people
would come together
—with everything
in creation—
assembling on the mountaintop,
to be with their origin,
and their source;

to be with God,
at the table,
that enormous table,
where everyone will find
a place,
>   *her place,*
>   *his place,*
>   *your place,*
>   *my place,*
in the house
of our Mother,
in the house
of our Father,
in the house,
of our Brother,
in the house
of our Sister,
in the home
of the Spirit of God.

4/3/88

21.

HIS GLORY AND WE

John 20:1-9

What had been hidden,
was now in the open.
What he had shown them once,
was now to be seen
all the time.
    Do you remember
    how he told the three,
    who had seen his glory
    on the top of the mountain,
    not to tell anyone
    about that splendor
    and that glory,
    before he would have risen
    from the dead?
An embargo
on the news
of the final outcome,
till he would have run
his course,
till he would have finished
his work.

He appeared to them.
He said:
"Peace,
peace be with you!
The peace I am in
now.
It will be
yours!
The transformation
I am now a lasting witness of,
it will be
yours!"
But leaving them there,
and leaving us here,
he made it clear,
that his peace,
that his transformation,
will only be ours,
once
we have run
our course;
once
we have finished
our work,
and not
before.

> We will not rise
> before we have died,
> we will not be glorified
> before we have lived,
> we will not shine
> before we have struggled
> with the dark,
> bringing it slowly
> to light.

As the Gospel of today explains:
"Till this moment,
they had failed to understand
the teaching of Scripture,

that he must rise
from the dead."
    Till that moment
    they had failed to understand
    that they,
    too,
    would have to be taken up
    in a process,
    in a life
    and in a mission,
    before they would be led to glory,
    after the work
    has been done,
    after the dark
    has been dispelled,
    after the past
    has been forgiven,
    and the present
    has been restored,
    after humanity
    has been brought
    together
    in harmony and peace.
They were still afraid,
of the world
as it was,
divided and ugly,
violent and corrupt
threatening them.
    They were still afraid
    of the evil,
    that killed him,
    while finishing his mission,
    while running his course,
    while being one with all,
    even with his enemies
    for whom he prayed,
    and for whom he died.

They were still afraid,
and they would be still afraid
for fifty days or so.
    But then they went out
    to preach and announce
    that we all belong together,
    in one glorious body,
    in the one family of God
    that will shine and shine
    for all ages to come.
They, too,
did not shine
before they had worked
at the love to come,
in blood,
tears,
and sweat,
by breaking the barriers
that still separate us
hindering the peace,
and the glory to come,
and we won't either.
    Those barriers
    will be broken through.
    He broke through them
    rising from his death,
    giving us the power
    to do the same,
    and rise like him
    in glory
    and light.
    Alleluia!

4/10/88

22.

IN HIS ABSENCE

John 20:19–31

Jesus appeared to them
over and over,
again and again.
In the one Gospel reading of today
he does it twice.
> Every time he appeared,
> he disappeared,
> and that is why
> he had to appear
> again.
Take the case
of Thomas.
> First he appeared to the other ten.
> Thomas was not there.
> Thomas did not believe them.
> Thomas wanted to make up his own mind.
> Thomas had to see him first,
> Thomas had to see him
> in his presence,
> before he would believe
> in his absence.

So he had to appear again,
to convince Thomas.
After his appearance to him,
he disappeared again.
        Why did he not stay with them?
        Why was he more absent
        than present?
Every time
he was recognized,
off he was.
        In a way
        the Easter story
        is much more a story
        of his disappearances,
        than of his appearances.
        The times he was away
        were considerably longer,
        than the times
        he was with them.
It was
as if he wanted to tell them
something.
It was
as if he wanted to tell them:
        "All right,
        I am alive,
        do not have any doubt
        about that,
        not even you,
        Thomas, dear.
        But I will be absent,
        I will be absent
        all the rest of your time,
        it will be
        up to you!"
                In the Gospel of today,
                he does not only
                tell them that.

He tells them, too,
what they should do.
How they should
react to that absence.
They should take over,
they should take up their responsibility,
they should be adults,
they should be entering the process
he had come to introduce
in this world.
They should no longer be
mere victims,
they should no longer be
passive observers,
they should no longer be
only objects,
they should be actors
and activators,
entering human history.
He blew
over them.
He said:
    "Forgive,
    change the shadows
    of the past!"
And before he left them
finally,
disappearing as dramatically
as possible,
endlessly high up
straight into the sky,
he told them
from above:
    "Go out
    into the whole of the world,
    and bring them all together:
    one Father,
    one Mother,

one Brother,
one Sister,
one Spirit,
the life of all!"
    Very many
    do not want to hear
    this news about him,
    this news about themselves.
Very many do
as if Jesus
did not leave.
    They are saying:
    "He is the answer!"
    They are saying:
    "He is my Savior!"
    They are saying:
    "He is my personal Savior,
    all will be right,
    maybe not now,
    maybe not here,
    but definitely then,
    and definitely there!"
And saying this,
they do not engage themselves
in this world,
really,
as he asked them,
as he commanded them
to do.
    We should never forget
    the message he gave us
    after his resurrection:
        "It is up
        to you!"
    That is why he blew
    over them,
    giving his Spirit
    to them,

before he left,
leaving us
in his absence,
as long as we will be
here in this world.

23.

BEGINNING FROM JERUSALEM

Luke 24:35–48

While the two from Emmaus
were still talking,
meeting quite some doubt,
and even unbelief,
he suddenly appeared
again
now in the midst of them.
    Even his appearance
    did not take their doubts away,
    they were too moved,
    they were too frightened,
    they were too surprised,
    they were too glad,
    Luke says,
    as if he had to apologize:
        "It was simply
        too much
        for them."
He respected their doubts,
he respected their unbelief,
he respected their fears,

that if he would be real,
their lives would have to change.
> So he proves,
> that it is he.
> He asks them
> to look at his feet;
> they come
> and bend over those feet.
> He asks them
> to look at his hands;
> they come
> and stare up at his hands.
> They see his feet,
> they see his hands,
> and not only that,
> they even see the traces
> of the wounds and the nails.

He then asks them
to touch him,
and again they come,
one by one,
hesitantly touching him,
feeling his hands,
stroking his cheeks,
laying their hands on his head,
and taking in his smell.
> Finally he asks of them
> a piece of fish.
> They pick a piece
> from the dish on the table,
> and give it to him,
> and while they watch,
> as they had watched
> so many miracles he performed,
> he takes the fish,
> breaking it,
> > —with a gesture
> > so well known to them,

    and so typically
    him—
putting it in his mouth,
chewing it,
and asking
for a second piece.
There is now no doubt
anymore
about him.
But so what?
What is the purpose
of this demonstration,
this object lesson?
    He starts to explain,
    how he fits in
    in the law of Moses,
    in the visions of the prophets,
    in the prayers of the psalms.
They begin to understand,
their faces change,
they do believe,
the old fascination captures them,
the influence he had on them before,
they do believe,
they do understand,
everything is all right
by now.
It is he,
as foretold
in the Scriptures!
    They are ready to go home,
    to their wives and their children
    to let them share
    in this good news about him.
    Everything has been clarified,
    he is dead
    but not dead;
    he belongs here;

and yet he is there,
he is safe and sane,
but appears now and then;
everything is all right,
and yet there is something so strange
about it all,
that they would like to be home
safely in bed
next to their wife
together with their children,
fast asleep till
the crow of the next cock
early in the morning.
They are ready to go,
the day has been very long,
the emotions too much,
the changes of events too fast.
They want to settle
as they were settled before,
though now immensely enriched
by the Jesus they met.
Let us go . . . !
He did not yet finish
He did not yet finish at all.
Again he calls their attention,
"This,"
he says,
"This is only the beginning!
I came to Jerusalem,
I died on the cross,
I rose from the dead,
to start a movement,
a movement
that should reach the whole of the earth,
a movement
that should cover the whole of the world,
a movement
that should touch the whole of humanity,

geographically everywhere,
socially all human affairs,
spiritually in the deepest of depths."
He looks at them
and he adds:
"Therefore,
I am sending you
on this mission,
if you want to be of me,
you should be with me;
if you want to be of me,
you can't settle now,
you will have to be on the move,
you have to be taken up in this process,
all the days of your life,
till the end of time!"
They were not supposed
to *have* their belief in him,
as you possess
something,
your money,
or your clothing,
your books,
or your nose.
They were supposed
to have their faith in him
as
a *dynamic force,*
as something
that made them move.
And so are we!
We who believe in him,
are often so happy
to be able to do that
even nowadays,
we are so content
to understand his role
in the history of the world,

that we think
that this is all
he could expect from us
in these our days,
and we settle in that belief,
we settle in this Jerusalem,
forgetting
that we should be
on the move
till kingdom come.

4/24

24.

KEEPING TOGETHER

John 10:11–18

"I am the good shepherd,"
he said
that day.
Just
close your eyes
and imagine a shepherd,
a shepherd
and his flock.
I do not know
what you see.
But I do know
that different people
would see different things.
      The shepherd in East Africa
      is often
      a small boy,
      with a stick in his hand,
      and the sheep around him.
The shepherd in many European countries
is an old man,

with gray hair and a beard,
a satchel on his side,
surrounded by dogs,
walking behind his sheep.

    In Jesus' country,
    even in our days,
    the shepherd is a very poor man,
    disregarded by all,
    very low
    on the social ladder,
    by the rich ranked among the scum,
    and walking in front of his sheep,
    guiding their way.

Here in the States,
the best picture most probably
would be
neither a child nor an old man,
but the cowboy,
not with his sheep,
but on a horse,
with his cows and his bullocks
all over the enormous prairie.

    In one thing
    all those shepherds are alike
    whether here or there,
    whether in our time,
    or in the time of Jesus,
    the main thing they do
    is
    keeping their flock together.
They take care,
not only of this one,
or that one,
but of all of them,
and if any one gets lost,
    —as Jesus
    so meaningfully
    explained—

they will not rest,
before they are all together
again,
the fat and the lean,
the white and the black,
the brown and the in-between,
the rams and the ewes,
the lambs and the yearlings,
being attentive to all.
It is with that task
that he was sent
in this world,
by his Father from on high.
It is with this mission
that he charged
each one of us,
in his turn.
We have to bring people together,
all of them,
without any discrimination
of race,
sex,
or rank,
being good shepherds of the flock,
even at the risk
of our lives.
We should be shepherds like that
in the families
in which we live,
feeling responsibile
for keeping all of them
together.
We should be shepherds like that,
in the schools
where we learn
or teach,
taking care
that no one is overlooked,

left out,
or lost.
We should be shepherds like that
in our business decisions,
at the boards we are on,
taking care
that we don't take for some
all the grazing there is.
We should be shepherds like that
while determining
whom to vote for
during whatever elections.
> We should be shepherds like that
> when determining our political stand,
> when evaluating the news,
> and reading our papers.
We should be shepherds,
keeping the whole of humanity
together,
and if anyone
is left out,
if any sheep would get lost,
if any lamb is overlooked,
we are no good
at the task
he wants us to be
as good at,
as he was,
a good shepherd
to all.
> If we are shepherds like that,
> if we are shepherds like him,
> God will be always
> with us,
> as God was
> and is,
> with him,
> and we will have nothing
> to fear.

May 1

25.

INTERCONNECTEDNESS

John 15:1–8

In the Gospel reading of today
Jesus tells us
of one of his experiences
in life.
He sees himself,
he explains,
as connected
with us,
as connected
with the whole of humankind,
as connected
with it all.
  I don't know
  whether you ever had
  that same type of experience.
  I don't think
  it is an experience unique
  to Jesus.
  So many people had it,
  I had it,

119

and I am pretty sure
that you had it,
too.
It is a feeling
that has been described
in very many ways.
It happens
in all kinds of circumstances.
I will tell you some,
and see,
whether you recognize it.
It is a very nice summer evening,
all is quiet,
you are standing in front
of a beautiful,
limpid lake,
the sun is just touching the horizon,
coloring everything
in a golden red,
you look out over the water,
and suddenly it is
as if all falls away,
the trees, the sun,the lake,
no,
it does not fall away,
but it is as if everything
is streaming in you,
or is it out of you,
and you feel
one with it all,
one with everything,
one with everybody.
Or you are listening to music,
it could be
the *Messiah* by Handel,
it could be
a beautiful piece of jazz,
and suddenly it is
as if you are taken up,

one with the music,
the trumpet takes you
out of yourself,
or maybe it is the clarinet,
or a saxophone,
and there is that feeling
that you belong
to the whole of the universe,
and the universe to you.
    Or you are looking
    at the one you love,
    and you get nearer and nearer,
    or you are sitting in a train,
    or in a plane,
    with all those people around you,
    as full of the wonder of the world
    as you are,
    all filled with potency,
    Spirit,
    and God-self.
Or you are just sitting at home,
knitting,
with the wool on your lap,
or you are doing the washing-up;
with the cat purring at your feet,
and again,
and again
it comes,
a sense of great contentment,
a great sense of belonging,
to the earth
and the sky,
to the sun
and the moon,
to the plants
and the animals,
to your family,
and all those you know,
and all those you don't.

Don't you carry in you
all human feelings?
Isn't that why you like
to read books,
watch a good film,
go to a concert,
or sing a song?
Today
he tells us
that he
had those experiences
just as we have them.
Today
he tells us
how he feels
connected with us,
as a vine
is connected with
the branches,
the leaves,
the flowers,
and the fruits.
Today
he tells us
that we have our home in him,
as he should have his home
in us.
The difference is,
that for him
all this was no vision
that passed
after some moments of insight
only.
For him it was not only a vision
that passed,
it was
and is the life he lived,
and lives,
always;

it is the life
he invites us to live
all the time,
   for ever and ever.
Our experience
of those moments
is right,
we belong together!
He with us,
and we with him.

26.

LOVING FRIENDS

John 15:9–17

The words Jesus speaks
in the Gospel of today
are so astounding
that nobody
ever seems to have dared
to believe them,
except some mystics.
Do you really believe
that God loves us,
as a friend!
And even if you think
that you believe
that God loves you,
do you really,
really,
think
that God loves
us?
    That is to say
    everyone
    in this world:

the Arab and the Jew,
the African and the Asian,
the Russian and the American,
the Northern Irish and the Southern Irish,
the Catholic and the Communist,
the Hispanic and the Amerindian,
the Pope and the President?
Don't tell me
that you believe that.
You don't.
We don't,
if we did
we would live
in a completely different world.
Those who believed in it
lived
in that different world.
I will give you
the example of someone
who did.
Her name is Etty Hillesum;
she was born in 1914
of Jewish parents.
She lived in Amsterdam
when the Nazis started
to arrest the Jewish population of that town
in view of their extermination.
Though she could have escaped
their fate,
at least for the time being,
she volunteered to join
the trapped Jews
in the concentration camp
Westerbork
from where the trains left
for the gas chambers of Auschwitz.
She found the courage to do all this
because she had discovered something
that she wrote in her diary,

—translated into American
under the title:
An Interrupted Life. *
She had discovered,
on New Year's Eve 1941,
the possibility of
"listening in"
to her inner self:
"A greater awareness
and hence easier access,
to my inner sources."
She noted
how she could get into contact
with her loving God,
not only in herself,
but also in everyone else.
"*Hineinhoerchen*
—I wish I could find a Dutch equivalent
for that German word.
Truly my life is one long hearkening
unto myself
and unto others,
unto God.
And if I say that I hearken,
it is really God
who hearkens inside me.
The most essential and the deepest
in me
is hearkening unto
the most essential and deepest
in the other."
It is because of this experience
of a loving God in everyone,
and in everything,
that she can even relate to her enemies,
her jailors.
God loves them all,
there is some eternity
in all of them.

"I love people so terribly,
because in every human being
I love something of You!
I feel a bond
with all your
warring creatures!

When her train left for her extermination camp
September 7, 1943,
she was in the company of
her father,
her mother,
and her sister.

She threw a postcard out of that train,
that was picked up
by a farmer
along the railway track.
He sent it on.
On it she had written:
"We left the camp,
singing."

Just before she had written:
"I wish I could live for a long time,
so that one day I may know
how to explain it,
and if I am not granted that wish,
then somebody else will perhaps do it,
carry on from where my life
has been cut short.
And that is why I must try to live
a good and faithful life to my last breath:
so that those who come after me
do not have to start all over again,
do not need to face the same difficulties.
Isn't that doing something
for future generations?"

She laid down her life
for her friends
because she loved them,
as the Father loves them.

She plugged into
the divine energy
that made the world
and keeps it together,
the love
that is the source of your
and my being,
a love
that is comprising
all.
When will we learn
our lesson?
When will our spontaneous reaction
be
his reaction,
who lived and died
for all?

*Hillesum, Etty. *An Interrupted Life: The Diaries of Etty Hillesum 1941–43*. New York: Pocket Books, 1985.

27.

GOOD NEWS

Mark 16:15–20

What is the *good news*
he spoke about,
before he went away?
  Was it maybe
  the fact
  that he would be away?
  Of course,
  it was not,
  and yet,
  sometimes I think,
  it was.
He was,
and still is,
the Son of God.
He showed that
in hundreds and hundreds of ways.
  He healed,
  and made people rise from the dead,
  He forgave,
  undoing the past;

he brought people together,
who had never been seen
together before;
he wrote in the sand,
and did not condemn;
he played his flute,
though nobody danced;
he provided bread,
and wine and fish,
and even a silver coin;
he was the master of animals,
of minerals and plants,
of the wind and the sea;
and during the night
he was with his Father,
often praying out loud,
as he did in the garden,
and when singing
his last song,
high on the cross;
he did all those things,
and once returned
from the darkness of death,
he said,
before leaving them,
that we all are like him,
that we all had his Spirit,
and we would be able
to do all those things,
and greater ones,
too.
And then he left,
neither with a bang
nor with a whimper,
neither stealthily,
nor unseen,
but in the open,
in the brilliance of a new day
straight into the rising sun,

until he could not be seen
anymore,
because there was that cloud
in which he disappeared,
or was he taken up?
   He left them alone,
   he left us alone,
   to be like him,
   and that is the news,
   the very good news.
It is through his departure
that he is showing us
that he really believes
what he said
about who we are,
and about what we would be able to do.
   Of course,
   he said,
   I am born from God,
   but aren't you?
Of course,
it is true,
the Spirit came over me.
Did he not come over you?
   Of course,
   I am the Son of God,
   but aren't you
   God's children, too?
Of course,
I carried my cross,
aren't you carrying yours?
   Of course,
   I rose from the dead,
   but do you think
   that you will sink away?
No way,
you will be there,
for ever and ever.
Amen.

All this reminds me
of an experience
you must have had, too.
You just learned something,
maybe to mow the grass,
how to drive a car,
or maybe ride a bike,
how to use a computer,
or anything like that.
Your instructor says:
"Okay,
I am leaving you now,
I think you can manage
on your own!"
But he does not leave,
though he is out of the room;
he is waiting out there,
to hear
whether you really
can do your job.
What a glorious
—and at the same time
frightening—
moment,
when finally you hear the outside door slam,
he is no longer there,
he is away,
he does trust
that you can do it
for yourself.
And that is what can happen
from that moment on.
He left them;
they were dazzled.
Was he serious?
Would they really be able
to live
like him?

They could not believe it,
but he did believe it,
he really left them.
> What a dramatic turn of events,
> what a change,
> what a chance,
> what a challenge:
> *good news*
> to all of them,
> *good news*
> to all of us.

We can do it,
whatever anyone else,
the Pope or the Bishop,
might say.
> We
> are equipped,
> we ourselves,
> to cast out the devil,
> to undo any evil,
> to tell the needed stories,
> to handle snakes,
> to neutralize any poison
> we might meet on our way.

Nothing can harm us,
no one can stop us,
we will overcome,
just as he did.
Alleluia.
Amen.

28.

HIS FEAR

John 17: 11–19

He was going home,
he was going where he had come from,
he was going to his Father,
he was going to leave them behind,
after having shown them
their power
in the Spirit.
    And suddenly it is
    as if he is gripped by fear,
    suddenly it is as if he is afraid.
    Was the Spirit
    he brought
    going to rip them
    apart?
    Was the Spirit
    he gave
    going to individualize them
    to the point
    that everyone would be privatized
    in herself,
    in himself,

     and divided
     from all the others?
It is the story
we hear so often.
It is the story
we hear all the time.
An apprentice comes in,
he learns the job,
techniques are revealed to her,
skills are taught,
the on-the-job training is very well done,
the expectations are great,
but then suddenly
he turns away,
she leaves,
with all that was learned,
with all that was shared,
to be on his own, her own.
     It is the story
     we hear so often,
     it is the story
     we hear all the time.
     The government put a lot of money
     into the training of a teacher,
     the scholarship was grand,
     the education great,
     the future very promising,
     the community eagerly waiting
     to profit
     from this budding talent,
     in which it invested so much.
     But after some time,
     after a year or two,
     the teaching job is left,
     the expertise used only for oneself,
     and in a way
     all effort and money
     is lost.
He had shown them
his Spirit,

he had shown them
their content,
their possibilities,
their potentialities;
what were they going to do,
how were they going to react,
would they use their newly discovered powers
for themselves,
as a dividing force,
directed against others,
exploiting others,
who had not yet made
that discovery?
>And he thought of Peter,
>and he thought of James,
>and he was must have been thinking
>of all future church leaders,
>of popes and bishops,
>priests and missionaries;
>he thought of you,
>and he thought of me.
Would they,
would we
be willing
to preach and to practice,
that all women and all men
have equal access
to divinity?
Or would they single themselves out,
because of the light they received,
leaving others in the dark,
to be able to rule over them,
as enlightened ones
almost always had done
in the past.
>Would they get "airs"
>because of the Spirit?
>Would they consider themselves
>as "the" chosen ones?

Would they use the "extra"
they were thought to have
to mystify the others,
their rights and their powers,
as the "world"
always had done,
again and again?
In front of them
he turned to his Father
and prayed:
    "Oh, let them be one,
    let them understand
    what I taught them.
    Let them not be divided
    against each other,
    because of what I revealed
    to them.
    Let them be one!
    Let them have the love and respect
    that only can safeguard
    the peace
    I came to bring them.
    Let them believe,
    so that they don't get lost!"
He turned to them,
he prayed to them,
too,
and he said:
    "Don't be like those
    of the world
    who use
    God's gifts
    of healing,
    and science,
    of legal insight,
    and business astuteness,
    to help themselves
    at the cost
    of others.

Don't be like those
of the world
who use
their God-given talents,
as if they
are the only ones
that count."
And turning to the Father,
he insisted again:
"Let them be one,
let them believe in me,
who did not come to be served,
but to serve,
as they should do,
though it is not
the way
of the world!"

29.

THE JESUS MODE

John 20: 19–23

They were sitting together,
after having cut off
the rest of the world.
Their doors were closed,
their windows, too.
They had to leave their house
now and then
to get some water,
to get some food,
a piece of soap,
the help from a doctor.
    They were glad
    to come back home
    to be in each other's company,
    to be with his mother,
    his "brothers and sisters"
    their wives, their husbands,
    and their children,
    eating and drinking,
    praising God
    and each other,

talking
and reminiscing.
And though they did not know as yet
exactly what it meant,
and how to do it,
they were breaking their bread
to commemorate him.
He had told them
to wait,
and that is what they did,
though they did not know
precisely,
what they were waiting for,
So they prayed,
and they ate,
they talked,
and they walked,
wondering
what he really expected
from them.
Then there was
that enormous fireball,
accompanied by that sound
outside.
At first it was one,
then it divided
and strangely enough
it descended upon
each one of them,
as if that fire
were not only one,
as they saw it above them,
but as if that fire
were one
even from within
all of them.
Suddenly they felt themselves
bound,
not only to each other,

but even to the ones
outside.
Peter burst through the door,
and to his own and utter surprise
announced:
          "The prophecies are fulfilled,
          God-Spirit speaks
          through each one of us,
          children and old people,
          the masters and the slaves,
          the Romans and the Greeks,
          do you understand
          what I said?
          We all belong
          together!"
                    Down in the street,
                    the same thing,
                    that had overcome the disciples
                    in that room,
                    happened now among them.
                    It seemed
                    that what they had heard
                    outside of them,
                    was coming from within,
                    and they said:
                    "We hear you speak
                    our language!
                    What should we do?
                    What is the meaning of all this?"
And Peter said:
          "Let us change,
          let us forgive and forget
          our past,
          let us be initiated
          in a totally new life
          with God the Father,
          who is parent;
          with God the Son,
          who is brother and sister;

with God the Spirit,
who is energy,
the life,
and peace in all."
That day
three thousand
accepted this word,
that came
from without,
and at the same time
from within.
A new type of human life,
the Jesus mode.

And now we are here,
in this church,
sitting together
after having cut off
the rest of the world,
as if nothing happened
to them,
as if nothing,
as if nothing happened
to us.
Aren't our doors closed
again,
and our windows,
too?
Would we be willing
to do
what Peter did,
just announce
from those doors,
and those roofs,
that the Spirit of God,
came over all
of them?

30.

TRINITARIAN DYNAMICS

Matthew 28: 16–20

Trinity Sunday
and many preachers today
will sigh and say:
>   "How can I preach
>   on a day like this?
>   What should
>   I say?
>   Who can fathom
>   the deepness of God?
>   Who can understand
>   God's names?
>   Shouldn't we leave
>   God's nature
>   just the way it is,
>   was,
>   and ever will be,
>   hidden and mysterious,
>   many and one,
>   Father,
>   Son,
>   and Spirit."

Preaching,
and reflecting on the Trinity,
is difficult
for another reason
also.
Meditating upon it
is not only reflecting
on God;
meditating upon it
is reflecting
on ourselves,
too.
Anything we say
about God
is something
we say
about ourselves.
Being Christians,
we are baptized.
We are baptized
according to a formula.
We are baptized
to be initiated
into a *new* life
where God is Father,
where God is Son,
where God is Spirit.
God
is not only Father
in God-self;
God
is our Father
too.
God
is not only Son
on God's own;
in Jesus God
became a brother
to us.

God
is not only Spirit,
in between Father and Son,
God
is Spirit
in between them
and in between us.
       That is what we believe,
       that is the core of our faith,
       that is what makes us Christians.
       It is because of this belief,
       we hold and maintain,
       that we are different
       from all the others
       around us.
It is because of this belief
that we say
that we live
in a Christian nation.
       It is the foundation
       of our democratic rights.
It is the explanation
of all our structures.
       It is even the reason
       that we are willing to fight,
       when our way of life,
       our rights and our freedoms,
       are threatened
       from within
       or from without.
Wasn't each of our wars
       —as our leaders
       do not stop
       to say—
because of that?
Aren't all our wars
       —as our church leaders
       so often stated—
Holy Wars?

In this nation
we believe
in ONE Father,
and you look at the world,
and see what we have
and others have not,
and you wonder:
one Father?
In this nation
we believe
in ONE brother,
and you walk through the streets
seeing the luxuries we can buy
with the money we have,
while others haven't the means
to buy their water and bread,
and you wonder,
one Brother?
In this nation,
we believe
in ONE Spirit,
and you look
at those who are participating
in services, education, and care,
and those who are not,
and you wonder:
one Spirit?
To believe in Trinity
is not to believe
in a thing,
an object,
a model,
a definition,
or an idol.
To believe in Trinity
means to believe
in action,
in dynamism,

in a revolutionary force,
in a liberation
that should change
the whole face
of this earth.
And if this belief
does not bring
that tension
with it,
why do you say
you believe?
May I ask you,
why?

31.

NOT YET

Mark 14: 12–16, 22–26

May I tell you a story,
a very simple story
about a soldier
during the First World War?
    I know,
    that is very long ago,
    but don't all stories begin with
    "Long, long ago . . ."
    to prepare us
    for the shock,
    that what they tell
    is really about us
    now?
It was October 16, 1916,
just before the battle of Douamont.
    In one of the trenches
    was a priest,
    his name was
    Pierre Teilhard de Chardin.
    He had a consecrated host
    with him,

in a small metal box
in one of his pockets.
Just before the battle started,
and just before he,
as a Red Cross soldier,
entered into action,
collecting the wounded,
and assisting the dying
as well as he could,
he suddenly got that desire
to be with Jesus
as united as possible.
Even the fact
that he had his presence
in his pocket with him
did not seem to be sufficient,
so he took the host
and gave himself communion.
Though he had Christ
now so near,
even in himself,
he felt that he should be
more one with him.
It was as if he felt still
a terrific distance.
In that state
he got a vision.
He saw in himself
the host,
and he saw himself
trying to take it,
but every time
when he had it almost in his hand,
the host receded from him,
out of reach,
as if to tempt him
to try again.
Then he noticed
something else.

Every time
he tried to get to Jesus
in that host,
and every time
he missed him,
he got something else in his hands:
    a wounded man
    to be dressed;
    a raving child
    to be helped;
    a friend
    to be consoled;
    a problem
    to be solved;
    a task
    to be fulfilled;
    a misunderstanding
    to be undone;
    a debt
    to be forgiven . . . .
Slowly
he started to understand.
Slowly
he began to see
what it all meant.
    He would be able
    to be one with Jesus
    only after having done
    all those things,
    after having fulfilled
    all the missions and tasks,
    his hands were filled with.
In between him
and his union with Christ,
was the distance
of the course
he would have to run
here on earth;

in between him
and his union with Christ,
was the mission
he had to fulfill.

      And with those thoughts
      he did not only enter the battle,
      but the rest of his life,
      a very difficult one,
      often in total loneliness,
      because of the visions he had,
      but sure up to the end
      in the reality
      of the body of Christ,
      which contained
      according to the vision he had
      the whole of humanity,
      the "total" Christ
      as he would say.

32.

THE LARGER CIRCLE

Mark 3: 20–35

His family got very upset.
They had heard
about his healing a leper
on a sabbath day;
they had heard
about his forgiving sins,
as if he were Yahweh,
they had heard
about his eating with sinners,
as if they ever did that;
they had heard
about his being surrounded by strangers,
so that he did not even have the time
to take his regular meals.
    They had come
    to take charge of him,
    a thing he
    so obviously
    was not able to do of himself
    anymore.

When they arrived in Capernaum,
at the place where he was,
their worst expectations,
and all those weird rumors,
proved to be true.
> They could not even get hold of him,
> because the house
> he was in,
> Peter's house,
> was not only full,
> it was surrounded
> by so many people around
> that they could not even get
> at the door.

They said:
> "We are his brothers,
> we are his sisters,
> this here is his mother,
> do you hear that,
> his mother,
> please,
> let us through,
> we are his family,
> we want to see him
> we have a right to see him!"

>> But no one listened,
>> nobody gave way,
>> it was as if they had lost him
>> once and for all.

They could hear,
now and then
some words from inside.
That is how they heard
that others, too,
considered him
to be mad,
or even worse,
that he was possessed
by a devil.

They tried to push,
to no avail;
the people around
simply did not let them through.
The only thing they could do
was send a message
from mouth to mouth,
saying:
> "Your mother,
> your brothers and sisters
> are outside at the door;
> they are asking for you!"
Even before that message reached him
they heard him say:
"A household
that is divided against itself
cannot stand."
Was he speaking about them?
They only wished
the very best
for him.
He should come back
in their circle,
he should not mix
with those others
> —who was this Peter
> anyway?—
he should stick
to their customs,
he should be faithful
to their rules,
he should respect
their taboos,
he should understand
his place in society,
he should take into account
the divine order.
> Finally the message
> seemed to have arrived,

because they heard him raise his voice
and say:
"Who is my mother,
who are my brothers,
who are my sisters?"
They could not believe
their ears.
Had he forgotten
all about them;
and then they heard him add,
obviously while he was looking around:
"All those here
are my mother,
my brothers,
and my sisters.
Anyone
who does the will of God,
that person is
my brother,
and sister,
and mother!"
He had broken the circle
of physical human relations,
he had broken the circle
of blood, race, and earth.
He spoke about a new family,
the family of God,
his family,
the family of those
who are brothers,
and sisters,
and friends,
not because they are born
out of the will of women and men,
but because they are born
out of God:
a Parent to all,
a Brother to everyone,
the Spirit with us.

P.S.
Did his mother understand,
or was she again just wondering
deep in her heart?
Later she definitely did,
and so did
James, the "brother" of Jesus
when he became
the leader of the first community in Jerusalem,
where the rest of his family
belonged to the same community,
after his return to the Father.

33.

WHILE HE IS ASLEEP (I)

Mark 4:26–34

There was a farmer,
there are millions of them,
who went into his field,
sowed his seeds
left, right, and center,
and went back home
after that.
> He never returned to that field,
> neither during the day,
> nor during the night,
> before harvesting time,
> trusting that in his absence
>> *—even*
>> while asleep—
> the seed would grow.
> And,
> it did;
> in the Greek text,
> a very modern word
> is used
> to tell us this.

The word is
automate
automatically!
Jesus sowed his seed
in our hearts
and off he went
like the farmer
of the story,
like farmers
all over the world.
Of course he knew
that things would not be ideal.
There were the birds,
and the droughts,
the weeds
and the insects,
the parasites
and the blights,
but there was also
the power of the seed,
maturing and growing
in humanity itself.
The divine power
will show its force,
and is doing that
all the time.
Sometimes we say,
that things are worse than before,
but we know
that it is not true,
they are better,
though not yet for all.
Think about the past,
the trading in slaves,
the horrors of child labor,
the nonrecognition of human rights,
the privileged very few,
and the miserable many.

Things are not worse,
but our expectations
are greater,
for the very good reason
that the seed has been growing
among us,
and it is still doing that,
there are so many examples of that.
> There have been
> very many famines in Africa
> but there has never been
> so much goodwill
> to finish that calamity
> before;
> there have been
> very many industrial injustices
> since the beginning
> of the Industrial Revolution,
> but there has never been
> a greater growth in the willingness
> to protect the poor
> before;
> land has always been stolen
> in South America,
> and elsewhere in the world,
> but the outcry against it
> has never been so loud
> before.
Don't tell me
that the seed is not growing;
it is.
And if you really seriously
do not think so,
is it not
because you yourself
are old and fruitless,
a barren part
in the human field;

a dry spot
in the human earth;
a stone
where others flower;
a dried-up yellow stick
where others bloom;
a moody grumbler
where others sing?
        Are you involved
        in the work of peace;
        are you engaged
        in the work of justice;
        are you a peacemaker
        in your community;
        are you actively taking part
        in political life,
        did you vote
        in the last election;
        did you opt for the poor
        at the last referendum;
        are you networking
        to stop the possibility
        of the nuclear blast?
If you are not,
you must be asleep.
His seed
did not grow in you,
as it did in his community,
or did not keep
abreast;
you are
out of tune.
Maybe you don't even know
about the last letters
from your bishops
about peace and justice.
No wonder
that you complain.

You are asleep
while the seed
is growing all around
you.
It is not you
who should be
asleep.
>He sowed
>his seed in us.
>He went away,
>knowing
>that one day
>we
>and you,
>too,
>would find that seed
>growing in us,
>through all the weeds,
>through all the droughts,
>through all the dangers,
>through all the blights
>and that we would be
>>*like a tree*
>>*that is planted*
>>*by water streams,*
>>*yielding its fruit*
>>*in season;*
>>*its leaves never fading,*
>>*and success*
>>*attending all we do.*
The outcome
is sure;
whether you will be part of it,
depends
on the growth of the seed
in you,
while he is away,
and asleep,

to wake up
at harvesting time.
    Grow with the rest,
    grow with the best!

34.

WHILE HE IS ASLEEP (II)

Mark 4:35–41

We are so strange,
we are so un-understanding,
we are so lazy,
we are so self-deceiving,
we are so unlike
he would like us to be.
Take the prayers
we say
for peace.
We direct ourselves
to God,
to Jesus,
often even not directly,
but through Mary,
Joseph,
or another saint
we trust.
We pray
and let all
depend on them.

We are surrounded
by a sea of missiles and bombs,
we hear daily the stormwind
of war-jets and star-fighters,
we all know
that tax money
is mainly spent
on the preparation
of an atomic hell
we all will be doomed
to be in.
Maybe we are even actually engaged
in the business of war,
working our projects,
screwing or welding
systems and parts,
and yet
the only thing
we do
for peace
is to bend our heads
and pray
to God.
Isn't that
what they did
when he was with them
in that boat,
with those waves,
and that water,
and wind
all around?
He was not afraid,
he trusted them,
they were the professionals.
He was so confident,
that he did not hesitate
to fall asleep
on that cushion
in the stern.

They were afraid,
they started to shout and to cry
like small children:
    "Help, help,
  we go under!"
        He woke up
        from his sleep
            —do you remember
            about that farmer
            and his sleep
            last week?—
        he looked around
        at the storm and the sea,
        and he did
        what they wanted him to do,
        he rebuked the wind,
        and he said to the sea:
            "Quiet,
            be still!"
The wind fell
and all grew calm.
Then he turned to them
and said:
    "Why are you so terrified?
    Why are you lacking in faith?"
        Did you ever reflect
        on the strange saying
        that came from his mouth
        that afternoon?
He could not blame them
for lacking
faith in him.
Hadn't they shouted to him
for his help?
Hadn't they waked him up
from his sleep?
They had a great faith in him,
they must have lacked faith
in something else.

They lacked faith
in themselves!
Instead of doing
what they could,
to get through the storm,
as they had done so often
before,
they had now called for him,
forgetting all they knew,
overlooking all their skills.
During that storm
in their time,
he interfered,
he was with them.
During our storm,
in our time,
he will interfere,
too,
but only through us.
It is up to us,
to calm
the storm;
it is up to us
to rebuke
the wind.
Let us not just
close our eyes,
and pray
to God:
"Does it not matter to you,
that we are going to drown?"
or
more appropriate
in our case:
"Does it not matter to you,
that we are going to blow up
and burn?"

35.

ON FENCING IN AND BREAKING THROUGH

Mark 5:21–43

The people around him
tried again and again
to fence him in,
to close the circle around
him.
> His family wanted him back
> in their homestead
> in Nazareth.
> His disciples would not allow
> children to approach him.
> The crowd around him
> told the poor and the blind
> in the gutters of the streets
> to forget about him;
> he had not come for them,
> they said.
> He was not supposed
> to talk to women in the street,

167

and definitely not
with the one at a well
in Samaria.
The Pharisees and scribes
wanted him to restrict himself
to them,
to the saintly
and the legally pure.
His disciples wanted him
to remain with them,
upcountry,
and when he told them
that he was going to Jerusalem,
they all advised him
against it.
He always escaped
those attempts.
He told his family,
not you,
but humanity
is my family.
He ordered his disciples
to allow the children
to come to him.
He stopped in the crowd
and asked them to produce
the poor and the blind,
who were shouting for him.
He talked with the women,
even the one from Samaria
at that well.
He sat down with sinners,
and with whomever those others
might have thought impure.
He left the countryside
and went to Jerusalem.
That trying to close
the circle

was not only something
that happened
then and there
around him.
It happens with us
when coming together
in his name.
We build a church,
     —though he never asked
     for buildings like that—
we start to know each other,
and we make coffee and tea,
a breakfast and doughnuts,
for after the Mass.
We organize
fairs and bazaars,
garage sales and cookouts,
barbecues and bingo sprees,
raffles and bull roasts,
and if we are not very careful
the circle closes
around us,
getting smaller and smaller,
often too small
for our young ones,
who escape
and leave.
He was not like that,
he was not like that at all,
he constantly fought against it.
     In the Gospel
     of today
     there is that woman
     who was bleeding,
     as she had been doing
     for over twelve years.
     This meant
     that she was impure,

      she had the type of impurity,
      the kind of contagion,
      that anyone who touched her,
      even unwillingly or unknowingly
      was impure and untouchable,
      too.
He did not seem to care,
he wanted the public to hear
that she had touched him,
because he knew
what had happened.
He had felt that power
going out of him,
and he wanted to teach them
a lesson,
the lesson
of widening one's circle
all the time.
      So she came forward,
      in fear and trembling
      while everyone
      was making room and giving way,
      so as not to touch her,
      but he even said
      that her faith
      had healed her.
He admired her,
an impure one,
he praised her,
a signed one,
a sick one.
They were amazed,
and scandalized,
just as we would be amazed
and scandalized,
if he joined us,
coming in with his friends,
the children and the poor,
the blind and the deaf,

the crippled and the mute,
breaking our circle,
because of his interest
and his love
not only for you
and me,
but for all of us.

36.

TOO MUCH FOR THEM

Mark 6:1–6

The rumor was there
before he himself.
He is coming,
he is coming.
> They all had heard
> about his miracles;
> they all had heard
> about his powers;
> they all had heard
> about his parables;
> they all had heard
> about his ideas,
> and now,
> finally,
> at last,
> he was coming,
> he was coming
> home.
He did not come alone,
what his family had told them
proved to be true,

they could see it now for themselves:
he was in the company
of followers,
young and old,
rich and poor,
as if he were
a rabbi.
    Sabbath came,
    they all went to the synagogue,
    and just as all had expected,
    some had hoped,
    and others feared,
    he started to speak.
    He taught in a way
    that really amazed them.
    That is why
    they did not even
    let him finish.
Where did HE,
that man they knew so well,
get that power?
Where did HE,
that one there,
    they had been working,
    they had been praying,
    they had been talking,
    they had been dancing,
    they had been quarreling,
    they had been walking
    with,
get those words from?
Wasn't he a carpenter?
Wasn't he the son of Mary?
Didn't they know
his brothers and his sisters?
    There was something strange
    about it!
    Didn't some scribes say
    that he was bewitched,

that he was possessed
by the evil one?
Hadn't his family gone after him,
because they thought
that he was out of his mind,
that he was mad?
How could
a common human being
like him,
an ordinary man
like themselves,
be like that?
Confronted with his power,
listening to the marvel of his words,
enjoying his stories,
seeing him there in the semidark
of their not-too-well-lit
synagogue.
full of majesty,
full of dignity,
full of divinity,
full of humanity,
full of Spirit,
they did not accept him.
They did not believe their eyes,
they did not believe their ears,
it could not be he,
he was just like
themselves,
and they were not like that.
They were just ordinary,
unimportant,
insignificant,
small provincial townspeople.
But so was he,
wasn't he?
He was just too much
for them.
They did not accept him,
but by not accepting him,

they did not accept themselves,
in their own possibilities,
in their own potentialities,
in their own humanity,
in their own divine origin,
either.
They were the victims
of an orchestration,
they were the victims
of an indoctrination,
that had been going on and on;
they were tied by chains
they would never be able to undo;
they had been labeled
too often
as useless,
as mean,
as low,
as nobodies,
by those who ruled
business, state, and temple,
that they could not believe
that neither they nor he
could be liberated
like that.
He had to be
as they saw themselves,
practically worthless
passive objects
in the history of humanity.
He could not be
what he pretended to be.
If he could,
should not they,
too?
Who could ask
a thing
like that?
So they threw him out,
preferring their status quo,

he was really
too much,
much too much,
for them.
>It must have saddened his heart,
>only some let him heal,
>having faith in him.
>And for the rest,
>he made his rounds
>in the villages about,
>preaching the *good news*
>of our liberation,
>that was too much for them
>at his home.

37.

SANDALS ONLY

Mark 6:7–13

Everyone knows
about religious leaders
and their powers
over others.
Who does not know
about the ninety-four limousines
of one,
and the enormous wealth
of others?
Who does not remember
the story
of the disaster in Jonestown,
somewhere in the South American jungle,
where hundreds and hundreds
decided to die
because of the whim
of one?
     Religious leaders
     do
     what lovers
     do
     to each other.

He says to her:
>"You made me
>a man,
>you made me discover
>myself!
>Thank you,
>I love you";

she says to him:
>"You made me
>a woman,
>you made me discover
>myself!
>Thank you,
>I love you."

Prophets bring people
to themselves,
they liberate,
they make people see.
That is what Jesus did,
that light in our darkness,
when he showed us by his life
what a human being
>—equipped
>with the Spirit of God—

can do,
and he said:
>"You will be able to do
>even greater things
>than I did!"

He made us
men and women,
he made us
discover ourselves.

>Do you remember
>how here in this country
>thousands would stand up
>under their leadership
>and shout:
>"We aren't a nobody,
>we are somebody!"

The ones
who can make people
do that
have to take care
that they do not abuse
the power
they have
to bring others to themselves,
undoing
what they seemed to do,
alienating them again
from themselves.
     And now he sent out his Twelve,
     to go and teach,
     to show and clarify
     how all of us
     are with God,
     and God with us;
     undoing the past,
     forgiving old sins
     and the long shadows
     they cast,
     chasing away devils,
     curing the sick,
     and bringing people to realize
     the Spirit in themselves.
Do you understand the power
and the might
messengers of that kind
have,
especially when they are really
sent out
by him,
Emmanuel?
     And so he warned them
     to take only a stick,
     and a pair of sandals,
          —those shoes
          that are quickly off,
          and as quickly on—

no luggage,
so that you can travel light
and move fast
from place to place,
stay in the same house,
until you move on.
With those rules,
it would be impossible
to fall into the trap
of trying to master,
to rule,
and to profit.
These prescriptions
can be clarified
by the rules for "evangelists"
in a booklet
Didache
or
The Teaching of the Twelve Apostles
written around the year 100,
that states
that an "apostle"
may stay for only one day,
maybe
for two,
but if he stays
for three days or more
then he is definitely
a false prophet,
out to have a good life,
profiting from his position
to rule
over others.
Even he did not come to be served,
he came to serve,
he came
to make us free,
to be ourselves
in the Spirit of God,

to make us
all we really are!
     Like any lover does,
     he did that to us,
     and we should follow
     his path.
     Are you doing that,
     going out as he did,
     going out like the Twelve
     he sent,
     unbinding others,
     healing them,
     anointing them,
     telling them who they are,
     making them
     all they can be,
     telling them
     about that Parent,
     about that Sister
     about that Brother,
     about that Spirit
     in them?
If you do,
then,
thank you,
I love you!
I see
dear Jesus' face
in yours,
I do!
Thank you!

38.

COME BY YOURSELVES

Mark 6:30–34

While he had a rest,
after having sent the Twelve out,
they had been very busy.
They had been traveling around
with their sticks,
and on their sandals,
eating what they found,
almost every night
staying in another house,
and waiting
in early morning
till the sun
had dried
the only tunic
they had been allowed to take,
still wet from its wash.
  They laid on hands,
  they healed,
  they anointed,
  they listened,
  they spoke,

182

they preached,
and they counseled,
all kinds of
physical, spiritual activities
they had never done before.
No wonder
they were tired,
no wonder they were glad
to be back,
totally exhausted,
while he obviously
was feeling very fresh.
       They told him enthusiastically
       about the work
       they had done,
       about the words
       they had spoken,
       but once the first enthusiasm
       was over
       they suddenly felt
       how tired they were.
A silence fell,
what would he say?
Send them on again?
Had they come back
too early?
Should they have
gone on?
       The work they had to do
       was very important.
       They had noticed
       that so well,
       when being out
       in the field.
       All those people
       who seemed so lost,
       strangers to themselves
       as sheep without shepherds,
       needed him,

and needed them
very much.
They looked at him,
and he said:
    "Come by yourselves
    to an out-of-the-way place,
    and rest a little.
    Let us go!"
        They took a boat,
        and off they went,
        and even before they came
        to the other side of the lake,
        most of them were fast asleep,
        so tired they were.
It was not only for that sleep
he had brought them over there.
Hadn't he told them:
    "Come
    by yourselves"?
They themselves
were more important to him
than the mission
he had just entrusted to them.
    Wasn't that mission
    precisely
    that everyone might come
    to himself or herself
    on their way
    to their inner being,
    where they would find God
    in the midst
    of themselves?
He heard the voices
of the approaching crowd
that had come around the lake
looking for them,
looking for him
in that very same search
for themselves.

They had been walking
as fast as they could.
It must have taken them
quite some time,
for they had about ten miles to go;
they, too, were tired,
dusty, thirsty, hungry,
and full of sweat,
after their effort
to be with him.
He sent his disciples away,
and he turned to the crowd,
looking so desperately for him,
but in fact
looking for themselves,
for their identity,
for the ones they were.
    And he took pity
    because they looked to him
    like sheep
    that had lost their way
    to the innerness
    of themselves
        —like anyone
        who
        runs after a guru,
        goes to a film,
        reads a book,
        travels to a strange country,
        or undertakes research
        in view of
        some enlightenment.
He turned to them,
and he said,
what he had told
his own chosen ones:
    "Just sit down,
    take a rest,
    and come by yourselves!"

That is what he taught them
that day
at great length,
to all
there,
and to us,
here.
Amen.

39.

OUR DAILY BREAD

John 6:1–15

For five Sundays
in a row,
we are going to listen
to the Gospel of John.
    According to many
    a Gospel that is very difficult,
        very mystical,
        overspiritual
        and allegoric.
That might be true,
but the five readings we start
today
are all about food,
    about bread
    about drink,
    about flesh,
    and about blood,
    and about things
    as concrete
    as all that.

It is never
about food for him,
it is never
about bread for Jesus,
it is never
about his drink.
Only once
is his bread mentioned,
and it was not even in John,
it was when Jesus
was hungry
after his fast in the desert,
and the one who spoke
was Satan,
who said:

    "You are hungry,
    I know,
    why don't you change,
    those stones here
    into loaves for you?
    There are plenty
    of them!"

When Jesus spoke
about bread,
it was always
about the food
others needed,
as in the reading of today.

    It was he
    who noticed
    that the children started to cry,
    that the grownups got irritated
    and started to yawn;
    it was he who saw
    that people were getting hungry,
    that no one was eating,
    that no one was drinking;
    and it was he
    who said to Philip,

   —poor Philip—
  "Where shall we find
  the bread
  for them to eat?"
For Philip the bread
was not the problem.
He knew from experience,
that you can go hungry
while the bakeries are full,
but you have no money
to buy any;
and it is still so true
today
of all those
who are hungry.
Our storehouses are packed,
our granaries overflow,
but the starving are too poor
to buy even a handful.
  So Philip said:
    "Not even the wages
    for half a year's work
    would enable you
    to buy the bread
    you would need!"
Then Andrew said
that there was
a boy
with some bread and some fish
he was willing to share
with Jesus
and the others.
  That small boy
  was willing to do
  what Jesus did,
  and what he made us
  all ask
  to be able
  to do

all the days
of our lives
sharing our bread:
    "Give *us* today
    our daily bread!"
That *us*
is not only Jesus,
that *us*
is not only you,
that *us*
is not only me
that *us*
is
all of us.
    So what should we do?
    Firstly,
    take care
    that we ourselves
    and those depending on us
    have sufficient to eat.
    Secondly,
    help those
    who are hungry
    far away,
    or very near to us,
    to get the food
    they need.
    Thirdly,
    work at the sharing of bread
    all over the world,
    by joining those who work
    with that aim,
    educating
    and lobbying
    to change our structures
    and economies,
    in such a way
    that Jesus' prayer,

and our prayer
is heard:
daily bread for the world.
Doing all that
we should not forget
that we
do not live by bread alone,
just as those
around Jesus
did not do
that day,
because they listened
to the words he said,
and they shared;
that small boy
being the first one
who understood,
what he meant,
but that is how children
are,
as Jesus so very often
said:
*Theirs is the kingdom
of heaven.*

40.

BREAD FOR THE WORLD

John 6: 24–36

Bread is very important,
bread is a principle
bread is a source,
bread is food,
bread is sustenance,
bread is holy,
bread is sacred,
bread is God's gift,
bread is God's grace
bread is from God,
bread is divine.
    One of the paintings
    one sees most often
    in the older American homes
    and presbyteries
    is a painting
    you can still buy
    in all sizes
    at the National Catholic shrine
    in Washington, D.C.

It is the picture of an old man,
with a beard and very gray hair,
who is sitting in front of a table,
with a bowl of soup,
a big piece of bread,
a knife and a spoon,
and a big book,
the Bible.
    He is praying
    before putting his spoon
    in the bowl,
    before putting the knife
    in the bread.
He is praying,
he is giving thanks,
the bread given
is life,
it was God who gave
that bread.
    No wonder
    that they came back,
    the day after he had given them
    all that bread.
They had not understood
that it was a sign
he had given to them.
They had not understood
how he had shown them
that they should be bread-
and life-giving
to each other,
just as he
and that small boy
    —who had suddenly appeared
    as a messenger
    from heaven,
    an angel—
had been to them,

giving them
all the bread and the fish
they had.

> That is why he told them:
>> "You are not looking for me
>> because you have seen a sign,
>> you are looking for me
>> because you want more bread."
> And they said:
>> "What are we supposed to do
>> performing the works of God?"
> And he said:
>> "Have faith in the one
>> God sent you.
>> Do what he does!"
> And they said:
>> "What do you do,
>> show us your sign,
>> give us our bread
>> just as Moses did."
> And he said:
>> "Moses did not give that bread.
>> God did that,
>> God gives the bread
>> that is life to the world."
> And they said:
>> "Sir,
>> give us
>> that bread always!"
> And he said:
>> "Don't you understand,
>> I am that bread.
>> Do as I do,
>> and no one
>> will hunger
>> or thirst
>> anymore!
>> Please,
>> understand!"

They were asking for bread,
they were asking for security,
they were asking for insurance,
they were asking for a permanent job,
they were asking him to take over,
they were asking him to be their king,
and he,
he never wanted to function
like that,
he wanted to be their model,
no more,
and no less.

     He wanted to be *their* bread,
          their principle,
          their source,
          their food,
          their sustenance
          their holiness,
          their sacredness,
          God's gift,
          God's grace.
     It would be
     up to them
     to be like him,
      bread for each other,
      bread for the world.
What we commemorate
in the Eucharist,
is more
than consolation
for our often
very sad hearts;
it is more
than comfort
for an often
very empty spirit,
it is
HE
in us,

sending us forth
to be in our turn
bread for the world
through our hands,
that became
HIS.

41.

DRAWING POWER

John 6: 41–51

According to the Gospel of today,
there is something mysterious
here in the world,
here in the church,
here in all of
us.
>It is mysterious,
>we don't see it,
>we don't smell it,
>we can't touch it,
>we can't hear it.
>It escapes
>our taste,
>it does not leave
>a physical trace.
It is there,
because
that is
what he said.
>There are many more
>of those mysterious powers

and energies
all around,
even through
and within us.
At the moment it seems to be
very quiet
in this church,
at least when I don't speak,
listen.
What do you hear?
Nothing,
silence.
But you know
that all this space around us
is full of waves,
energies, and powers.
Were I to switch on a radio
here in this church,
where it is now so still and quiet,
suddenly music would burst forth
out of this audible silence:
hard rock,
country music,
monks singing plain chant in a convent,
a symphony orchestra from Montreal,
and voices from all over the world,
from Peking and Moscow,
from Holland and Japan,
from Rio de Janeiro and Djakarta,
from Lagos and Cape Town,
from San Francisco, New York,
and Baltimore.
    That power is there,
    those vibrations are present,
    all that energy is hovering around.
The gospel today is about
another type of mysterious energy:
a divine one,
a terrific one,

a mighty and powerful,
an all-explaining,
an all-unifying one.
It is there,
while it does not seem to be here
at all.
Jesus calls it
a drawing power.

It is a power,
an energy coming from God,
attracting all of us,
the whole of creation,
through Jesus
to God.
That there is a
drawing power
in nature
is clear:

things are born,
trees grow up toward the light of the sun,
plants are flowering,
fish are swimming,
insects are crawling,
birds are flying,
animals of all kinds
are roaming around
looking for an equal,
searching for a mate,
getting offspring.
Adam embraced Eve,
and Eve embraced Adam,
boys kiss girls
and the clouds are perpetually
chasing each other.
But Jesus speaks
about a power
that draws all of us
to him,
and at the same time,

also,
of course,
to each other.
>Protestants and Catholics,
>Christians and Hindus,
>Muslims and Jews,
>Americans and Russians,
>Asians and Europeans,
>aren't we all communicating
>and dialoguing
>more than ever before?
There is a power
all around us.
It is changing
the face of the earth.
Jesus did not reveal only
its nature,
but even what its outcome
would be:
>It is the
>*drawing power*
>of our origin,
>our Father and Mother,
>attracting us
>to her home,
>to his table,
>to the table and the home
>we all are coming from.
We are surrounded by that power.
It is all in
and through us,
it explains
why you,
why I,
why we,
have that deep,
deep feeling,
that the world in which we live
is not all there is,

that the colors we see
are not all the colors there are,
that the sounds we hear
are not all the music and language there is,
that there are other recipes for the food we eat
than the ones we know,
but much more important,
that the relations we have,
that the ways we touch each other
do not fulfill all our desires and hopes,
in one word:
> that the love we meet
>> —and that love
>> can be so great,
>> so fulfilling
>> and consoling—
> is a mere beginning,
> giving us only an inkling
> of the time
> when God's drawing power
> will have brought together
> feasting and celebrating
> the kingdom of God,
> the fullness of the life,
> the glory and the power
> given to us.

Jesus gave the lead,
so let us
plug in,
becoming all
we really are.

42.

DO YOU LOVE ME?

John 6: 51–58

They had come to him,
because he was their provider,
their baker,
they wanted his bread,
because it was cheap,
they wanted his bread
for nothing.
    They had come to him,
    neither because of him,
    nor because of his words,
    his expectations,
    his hopes,
    or his dreams.
They had come to him
not because of his person,
but because of what he had.
    He understood,
    and he made the complaint,
    so often heard
    in books
    and in plays,

in tragedies
and in dramas,
so often heard
in the run
of our everyday lives:
    she and he sit together,
    being out,
    in candlelight,
    they dined very well,
    and costly, too,
    he pays,
    and he says to her:
    "Do you really love me
    or do you only love
    the things that I have,
    my car outside,
    the diamond I gave you,
    the food we ate,
    the dances we danced
    the kisses I kissed,
    do you love me,
    do you really love me,
    or is it only all that?"
And she in her turn,
asks him
that question
as old as human love:
    "I know
    that you love my looks,
    my hair,
    my kisses,
    and my hugs;
    I know
    that you love the way
    I dress and undress,
    but do you really love
    her,
    within that dress,
    me,

the one my body
is?"
The question
is asked
by her
and
by him,
by lover
and loved one,
by loved one
and lover.
The question is double
the question is two.
And just as all of us
would,
Jesus is wondering
about them.
Did they come
for the bread
or did they come
for him?
Did they understand
that *he*
wanted to be their bread?
Did they understand
that *he*
wanted to be the reason
for their love?
They in their turn
must have been wondering
about him;
and we might
or even should
do the same.
The question is double,
the question is two.
Did he really come,
because he loved
them?

Or did he only come
because he needed
them,
to realize his dream,
God's kingdom
here
on earth?
Does he need us,
or does he love us?
Did he come for me,
did he come for you,
in view of others,
or did he come for me,
in view of me,
and for you
in view of you?
Our question
is just as valid as his,
his question
is just as valid
as ours.
In the reading of today
he gives his answer.
It is a classical answer,
too.
The classical
human answer,
but now divine,
coming from God,
the mysterious
and sacred source
of us all.
Isn't the human answer,
an echo,
a shadow,
a replay
of what God
said of all of us
from the very beginning:

"Remain in me
and I will remain in you."
Lovers hope it,
lovers plead for it,
lovers are looking for it,
all the time:
Remain in me,
and I will remain in you.
Lovers say it,
lovers promise it,
lovers believe it,
all the time.
"Let us be together,
let us be one."
All lovers do,
all friends,
too,
but even the best of lovers,
even the best of friends,
remain at a distance,
remain strangers,
remain people
with their own feelings,
with their own thoughts,
with their own worries,
with their own hopes,
with their own spirit,
with their own heart,
with their own flesh,
with their own blood.
Human friends do,
but *he*
isn't only human,
he is divine,
he can come
to the center
where we started
and live,

he can be present
without any limit.
That is why
it is so very good,
so unbelievably good,
so immensely good,
to hear him
say:

> *"Remain in me,*
> *and I will remain in you!"*

What else
can a lover,
what else
can the loved one,
what else can we
ask
or hope for?

43.

EATING HIM

John 6: 60–69

For the pious Hebrew
the law,
the Torah,
was like bread.
It was something
to be eaten.
They should have it
in their mouth,
the first psalm says,
just the way Jeremiah did,
    "chewing
    and digesting it
    as a lion
    its prey."
        It is how Jesus
        the new law
        should be
        now for us,
        chewed and eaten
        swallowed and digested
        flowing into us,

assimilated,
supporting us
in all we do.
Who really would want that?
They were
and they are
so few.
Too many of us
are too tired
too fatigued,
and too frustrated
to listen to all this.
It has been so often preached,
it has so often been tried,
it has so often failed.
They sigh
and sit in front of the TV or VCR,
they listen to the radio or compact discs,
they read the papers,
their *Newsweek* and *Time*
to see,
to hear
that today again
it is worse
than the day
before.
"There is nothing new
under the sun,
there will never be anything new,
vanity of vanities,
all
is vanity!"
Isn't it better to lie down
than to sit up;
isn't it better to sit up
than to stand?
Isn't it better
to be dead
than to be alive?

Others escape
by living only for today,
they are out for each pleasure
they can get out of this moment,
always on the lookout
for new things,
a new gadget,
a new taste,
a new color,
a new fashion,
a new sound,
a new whatever.
It is definitely better to live
than to be dead,
pick any day that comes,
sit in the sun
and enjoy
God-only-knows-what
the morrow will add.

    And then there are those
    who are eating him,
    in that old way of Psalm One,
    and who consequently
    are eaten by him.
    They are few,
    but they are there,
    they are the ones
    who did not leave him,
    and who are enthusiastic
        —that means
        full of Spirit—
as he is and was.
Believing
in God's drawing power,
believing
in God's love,
believing
in a growth
and a mission,

the realization of God's kingdom
here on earth,
and in heaven.
They ate him,
and they eat him,
living
on his blood,
on his flesh,
on his words
of eternal life.

44.

KILLING LAWS

Mark 7: 1–8, 14–15, 21–23

They had come all the way
from Jerusalem
to catch him.
Not out of love for God,
not out of love for God's law,
but because of their hatred for him,
as he threatened to undermine
their power
over the crowd.
> They had been watching him all day,
> they had not been able
> to find in him anything wrong.
> Obviously he was an observer of the law,
> in dress,
> in words,
> and in his behavior.
They stopped looking at him,
they gave up on him,
they started to observe his followers,
that ignorant bunch,
who were no longer listening to them,

but who were following him,
as if they had found a new leader,
as if they did not exist
anymore.
  They looked on
  and they watched,
  and finally they caught some
  who did not wash their hands
  before they started to eat,
  as required by their custom
  and law.
Why hadn't he warned them?
Why hadn't he reproached them?
Why did he let this pass
without a word?
They attacked
in the name of their law,
they attacked
in the name of their prestige
and their power.
  They did not appeal to that law,
  to create space and freedom;
  they did not appeal to that law,
  to guarantee or improve the human lot;
  they did not appeal to that law,
  to enable life and joy;
  they did not appeal to that law,
  to enhance or celebrate;
  they did not appeal to the law
  out of love for God;
  they appealed to it
  to litigate and win,
  to profit and to gloat,
  to catch and to kill.
He looked at them
with their faked pious faces,
he looked at them
full of hatred and greed,
and he said:

"You hypocrites,
how far are God's intentions
from your hearts;
how false is the reverence
you seem to pay.
Is that God's command,
to catch and to kill,
to hunger and to lust,
to rule and to reign,
to exploit and to plunder?
You say
that you stand for justice;
you say
that you defend God's will;
but you only intend to profit yourselves,
at whatever the cost."
He did not say
that the law is no good;
he did not say
that the law should be abolished;
but he did say
that day,
that law can be used in such a way
that it kills,
that it stinks,
that it makes human life
impossible.
It does.
It does
in the most literal sense
of the word.
Did you ever hear
how difficult it became
to get some help
and assistance
in the case of the birth
of a new human life
among us
in certain states?

Did you ever hear
that doctors and midwives,
obstetricians and gynecologists
are so afraid
of a natural happening
like a birth
that they do not dare to take the risk
of assisting anymore,
because they might be sued
if anything would go wrong
and they cannot pay the insurance
against it anymore?
Did you ever hear
how fewer and fewer people
want to stop
at an accident along the road
that they are driving on,
because
if you get involved
and make a wrong move
you might be sued
for the rest of your days?
Jesus' words are a warning for us.
If we do
what those people from Jerusalem
did,
watching if anything
might go wrong
according to the letter of the law,
to catch
and to fleece,
we are not sincere;
we are hypocrites,
making human life
impossible.
Even a good thing
like the law,
even an excellent thing
like God's law

can degenerate
in the hands of people
to something
that kills,
as it did
in the case of Jesus
himself,
when they nailed him
on the cross
in the name
    —so they
    said—
of God's law.

45.

THEY BROUGHT HIM A MAN

Mark 7: 31–37

They brought him a man,
who was deaf,
and consequently
could not speak very well.
>It is not said
>that he himself went,
>not even that he wanted
>to go,
>he was brought.
Was he pushed?
Was he pulled?
Was he forced?
>Did they treat him
>as an equal,
>or did they treat him
>as we so often do
>the disabled
>among us.
Did you never notice
how disabled persons
are overlooked
and the *bystanders* are asked:

217

"What does
he want;
what does
she want?"
as if they would not be able
to speak for themselves
or make up their minds.
    Then why did they bring him?
    Was it to help and support him,
    or was it
    because they wanted
    to use him
    as a kind
    of guinea pig,
    to see whether Jesus
    would heal,
    and to have
    a free and brilliant show,
    something they would be able
    to tell all around,
    saying they had seen it,
    by themselves?
They brought him
before Jesus,
harassed,
embarrased,
hopelessly shy,
frustrated,
hearing nothing
of what they said,
and not able to utter
a single word.
    Jesus took him
    aside,
        —thank God,
        the deaf man
        thought—
    far from the crowd,
    around the corner of the street,

behind a bit of bush,
and he told
the crowd
to remain behind,
on the place
where they were.
When they were
by themselves
        —as he later
        was able
        to tell—
they started
to communicate
in the only language
we *all* know,
that of signs.
        Jesus touched his ears,
        the man made a sign,
        that they were useless,
        and Jesus
        spat on the ground,
        Jesus touched his tongue,
        the man made a sign,
        useless,
        too,
        and Jesus did
        what the man had done,
        all through his life,
        he groaned and sighed.
The man must have felt understood,
his fear was melting away,
he almost *heard*
what Jesus had done,
finally someone
who sympathized;
finally someone
who took him seriously;
finally someone
who took his side,

who did not want to use him,
or play a trick,
or make him the centerpiece
in a show,
or a demonstration.
>   The circle
>   that always enclosed him
>   already started to open,
>   his isolation was over,
>   he started to hear,
>   he began to understand,
>   a miracle was going to happen.
>   It had happened already!
>   He saw Jesus look up
>   to heaven,
>   he did the same,
>   he looked up,
>   he saw Jesus
>   sigh,
>   and so
>   did he.
He was no longer alone
he saw,
no,
he heard,
he heard him say:
>   "*Ephphatha*
>   be opened!"
He was opened up,
he was freed,
he was unbound,
he was liberated,
he was healed,
they together had prayed,
and their prayers
had been heard.
>   Together
>   they reappeared
>   from behind the bush,
>   around the corner of the street.

The crowd was still there
eagerly waiting.
They saw them speaking
with each other,
they saw them listening
to each other.
They were amazed,
beyond themselves,
and they did
what they should have done
long before,
as we should do
every time
we meet a person
like that.
They received him
as an equal,
healing him
in that way
from all
that is
evil.

46.

HE STARTED TO TEACH THEM

Mark 8: 27–35

That morning
they set out again
with him,
as they were now accustomed
to do.
    It had become
    a regular pattern
    in their lives,
    they had become
    quite settled
    in his company.
It was nice,
it was pleasant,
sufficient to eat,
plenty to drink,
taxes paid,
respect
and a good reception
almost everywhere;
a miracle here,
a wonder there,
signs of greater things to come,

basking in his glory,
interesting conversation,
beautiful stories,
thrilling discussions,
plenty of self-expression,
they never had been so contented
during all their lives;
they never had had it
so good.
Insofar as they were concerned
it might last
for ever and ever.
They seriously started to consider
making their following him
a second career.
        When he turned to them
        asking:
                "Who do people say
                I am?"
        there was no hesitation,
        they had given him
        an honest answer,
                —though they thought
                they knew better—
        they had answered:
        "Some say John the Baptizer,
        others Elijah,
        and again others
        one of the *prophets*."
When he asked them again:
        "And who do you say
        I am?"
they looked at each other,
they looked at Peter,
they gave him a wink,
that he should tell him,
and Peter said:
        "You are
        the Messiah!"

That is what he said,
that is what they thought
he was.

> "The promised one,
> who will march
> the whole of the people
> toward glory and victory,
> and we will be there
> in front with you,
> you bet!"

That is what he did not say,
it is what they thought.

> He now fully turned to them,
> and he told them,
> that they were right,
> but that the people were right,
> too.

He was the Messiah,
he was also a prophet,
as the people had intuited.
He would be treated as one of them.
And he told them
how he would be rejected

> by the elders,
> by the chief priests,
> by the scribes,
> and finally by his own people

as all the prophets
and prophetesses
had been in the past,
how he would suffer,
tortured and beaten,
humiliated and spat at,
naked and raw,
crucified and murdered,
though

> —he added—

he would rise
three days later.

Again they looked at each other,
they looked at Peter,
they gave him a wink,
and this time
Peter took him apart,
to tell him
that they did not agree,
that this should not happen,
neither to him,
nor to them.
Peter said:
      "Forget about those prophets,
      forget about what the people say,
      forget those ideas,
      bc glorious,
      be victorious,
      be the Messiah,
      be the one
      we think
      you are!"
He turned against Peter,
he turned against them,
and he said:
      "Satan,
      get behind me,
      follow me!"
Then he called
all the people together,
he told them
that they were right,
he told them
you can't be my follower
without understanding
that you would have to take up
your cross,
as all the prophets had done,
and as he was going to do,
going to Jerusalem,
he told them,

that you would have to forget
about your own life,
if you wanted to save it.
He told them:
    "If a person wishes to come after me,
    he must disown himself,
    carry the cross,
    and walk in my footsteps.
    Whoever would save his life,
     will lose it,
     while whoever loses his life
    for me and the gospel,
    will save it."
He asked them,
to be prophets,
he asked us
to be like
him.

47.

ON IMPORTANCE AND RANK

Mark 9: 30–37

From then on
he taught them
while they were
on his
and their way
to Jerusalem.
 First he spoke
 about his death;
 death,
 the great equalizer,
 death,
 that would make him
 equal to them
 and to us.
Hearing him speak
about his death,
they started to speak,
about their inequality
 —was it in view
 of his death,

and their succession
to him?
They were discussing
importance and rank.
Who among them was first,
who second,
who third,
and who would be
the last one,
the unhappy one,
number thirteen,
13.
They were looking
for a measure,
for a criterion,
for a norm,
was it initiative,
was it Peter,
was it friendship,
was it John,
was it business-mindedness,
was it Philip,
was it political insight,
was it Judas Iscariot,
was it money,
was it Matthew,
was it blood-relatedness,
was it James,
was it mercy,
was it the other Jude,
was it justice,
was it fame,
what was it,
who was it?
They did not know.
They came home,
they sat down,
he sat down,
too.

He asked them:
    "What were you
    arguing about
    on the way?"
They did not look up,
they did not look at him,
they looked at their knees,
and the earth
in front of them.
He went out,
through the open door,
in the street,
where you could hear
the noise of playing children,
and he brought in
one of them,
    a small little girl,
    wide-open eyes,
    with a star of light in them,
    a snotty nose,
    a bunch of pitch-black hair
    and rather dirty feet.
        He put that child
        in the middle of them,
        and he said:
    "Anyone
    who takes in
    a child like this,
    considering it
    as important as oneself,
    is taking in me,
    and whoever takes in
    me,
    is taking in
    the One
    I am coming from!"
So that child,
is as important
as God,

and who could be
more important
than that?
> They looked at the child,
> they looked at each other,
> they looked at him,
> they understood,
> though they often
> > —very often—
>
> would forget.

Aren't we
all of us
like that child,
the center of God's
and of Jesus' love,
and is the lesson not
that we are all
> —all
> of us—

equally important,
the most important?
> Isn't that dogma
> the key
> to redemption,
> to liberation,
> to justice
> and to peace?
> Isn't it the fundamental reason
> for our interest
> in disarmament,
> in anti-apartheid,
> and in a just
> and equitable
> social structure?

He patted the head
of that little girl,
who laughed
and giggled,

leaving the darkness
of their room
for the bright sun
and its play
in the street.

48.

ON EQUALITY

Mark 9: 38–43, 45, 47–48

They came to him
full of indignation.
They had seen a man
expelling demons
in the name of
Jesus.
    They had tried
    to stop him,
    because he had never been
    sent out by Jesus,
    he did not even
    belong
    to their company!
If things like this
would be permitted,
where would
their own prerogatives
be?
What would be the difference
between those who had seen
and those who did not;

between those who had heard,
and those who had not;
between those who had been present,
and those who had been absent;
between those who had been touched,
and those who remained untouched?
    They tried
    to make themselves
    different
    in his name!
They tried
to reserve
healing and salvation,
exorcism and forgiveness,
for themselves
in his name!
    They wanted
    to be seen
    and to see themselves
    as more important,
    as more equal,
    than all the others
    in his name!
They wanted
at that time already
to be called
masters,
reverends,
monsignors,
worships,
holinesses,
and fathers
in his name!
    They wanted
    to be,
    and to be seen as,
    superiors,
    in his name!

Maybe they had started
already
to dress very differently
from all the others,
in his name!
    They definitely had forgotten
    almost immediately
    the lesson
    he had taught them
    with that child
    in the center of their circle,
    telling them,
    that God,
    and he himself,
    was as much with that child
    as he was with them.
He repeated his lesson,
and he said
that anyone
who would do even the simplest deed
    —like giving
    a cup of water—
to one in need
in his name
would be acknowledged
and rewarded
just as
they would
when doing
their greatest of goods.
    He added
    that anyone
    who would teach differently,
    that anyone
    who would introduce
    or make differences,
    that anyone
    who would lead others astray
    on this point,

making others think
of themselves
as unworthy,
insignificant,
or small
would not escape
punishment.
It would be better,
he said,
that those who teach
something like that
be plunged
in the sea
with a great millstone
fastened
around their neck!
So beware,
he told them,
beware,
do not divide,
do not discriminate,
do not classify,
do not make differences,
beware,
do not divide
what God made
one
and
equal.
If you do,
you will be punished,
you will
perish!

49.

ON MARRIED LOVE

Mark 10: 2–16

The Pharisees
came to test him.
>Was it to put him
>in difficulties
>on an issue
>that had caused
>the execution
>of John the Baptist?
>Or was it to catch him
>on a cause
>that was then,
>as it is now,
>very delicate?
We don't know.
We only know
that Jesus,
in his turn,
put them
to the test.
We also know
that they failed it.

When he asked them:
"What command
did Moses give you?"
they answered:
"Moses permitted divorce,
and the writing
of a divorce letter."
He did not agree,
he did not agree at all.
He told them:
"That is not
what Moses did,
he *obliged* you
to write such a letter,
because of the hardness
of your hearts."
     Moses had
     a very good reason,
     to prescribe
          —"in God's name"—
     that obligation.
     An obligation,
     in that time
     when hardly anyone could write,
     was a rather complicated
     affair,
     almost equal
     to a legal procedure
     nowadays.
Before that law,
and even after it,
men had been accustomed
to send their wives away
for the smallest and strangest
of reasons,
a badly cooked meal,
a sickness,
age,
being bored,

having fallen in love
with someone else,
and things like that.
That is why
Moses had put them
under the obligation
of a formal dismissal letter,
to protect
at least somewhat
the rights
of the women.
>   That is why Jesus
>   insisted:
>>   "He did not *allow*
>>   you
>>   to write
>>   such a letter,
>>   he *obliged*
>>   you."
And then
he adds his own reason
to tell them
that this cannot be done.
A woman cannot be disposed of
as if she were
something
you can throw away
when you have used
it,
just for lust,
or to perpetuate
your name!
>   He says:
>   "This relation
>   between husband and wife
>   is such
>   that the two
>   form
>   one flesh.

Therefore let no man
separate
what God has united."
Isn't this what all couples
hope,
at the moment
they stand
in front of the altar,
surrounded by their communities,
saying:
    "Yes, I will!"
    "Yes, I will!"
    That hope is sincere,
    it is their promise,
    it is their prayer,
    it is their blessing.
        Yet,
        seven out of every twenty couples
        who stood next to each other
        promising it,
        hoping for this grace,
        will be divorced
        within ten years,
        here in this country,
        here in the States,
        and sometimes
        in some regions
        the proportion
        is even
        twelve out of twenty.
Hopes not fulfilled,
prayers not heard,
efforts in vain,
promises unrealistic,
frustration,
disaster,
a curse
instead of
a blessing;

death
instead of
life.
     Does this mean
     that in those cases
     the two
     really became
     one flesh?
Should those couples
remain together?
Did he really want
situations
to continue
like that?
     Jesus said:
          "They shall
          become
          as one,"
     but does it always
     happen like that?
Let us pray,
and let us hope,
that it will happen
to our children,
in view of themselves,
in view of our grandchildren.
Let us hope and pray
that it will happen
to all those we love.
Let us pray,
and let us hope,
that we ourselves
     —married or
     unmarried—
will never find ourselves
in the case
that a letter of dismissal
would be
the only way
out.

Because it is true,
it is God's divine ordinance,
it is the way we are created:
every woman,
every man,
needs
someone
to be whole,
and to become one
in the human
flesh.

50.

ON SELF-LOVE

Mark 10:17–30

He came jogging,
he came
jogging for his life,
as joggers do.
It does not say
where he came from.
It does not say
where he went to,
he ran
as joggers do.
    He stopped
    for a moment,
    he fell on his knees
    before him,
    and he said:
        "Sir,
        what should I do
        to share
        eternal life?
        What should I do
        to find it all?

What should I do
to love
completely?"
Jesus looked at him,
and he gave him
the common answer,
the normal way out,
though everyone knows
that it is neither the final answer
nor the final solution.
He said:
"Do not kill,
do not commit adultery,
do not steal,
do not testify falsely,
do not deceive,
honor your father and your mother. . . ."
Before he even finished,
the young man replied:
"I did all that,
I did it from my youth,
but I know
that it is not sufficient,
that it is not all!
What more
should I do?"
Again he looked at him,
and said:
"If you really
want to share
in eternal life;
if you really want
to share in it all;
if you really want
to love completely;
if you really want
the kingdom of God,
loosen yourself
from all you have,

sell it,
give it away,
and once free,
totally free,
come to me
and be
as I am."
That man looked up,
no,
it was I
who looked up,
no,
it was you
who looked up,
his face fell,
my face fell,
your face fell,
and he,
and I,
and you
went away
sad,
knowing that what he asked
was something
we could not do
as yet,
not ready to come,
not ready to grow,
not ready to enter,
and we ran on,
and we are jogging still,
having with us
that same question;
having with us
that same desire
all the time.
We should
never forget
what that young man
never forgot,

neither those who were
witnesses to the scene
nor the one who informed Mark about it,
who noted so carefuly,
how Jesus remained looking
after him,
with love
and with a smile.
Just as he is looking
after you,
and after me,
saying
to his amazed disciples;
　　"For a human being
　　it is impossible,
　　but not for God!
　　With God
　　all things are possible."
It is that love,
it is that smile,
it is that promise
we will find,
when our running
is over
when our jogging
is done,
I trust.

51.

ON GREATNESS AND BEING OF SERVICE

Mark 10:35–45

"The Son of God
has not come to be served,
but to serve,
 he gave his life
 in ransom for the many."
  When meditating
  on these words
  we should not think only
  of his death.
  We should think of him
  all during his life.
That is why
he was born,
fled to Egypt,
grew up in Nazareth,
was baptized by John,
prayed and fasted
in the desert,
started his public life,

worked miracles,
chased evil,
taught and preached,
had no time to eat,
had no place to sleep,
contacted others,
calmed water and wind,
and ate with saints and sinners,
sharing with them
his glory.
>   That is why
>   he was finally arrested,
>   put before court,
>   crowned with thorns,
>   scourged,
>   dragged through the streets,
>   nailed to the cross,
>   and pierced with a lance
>   while dying.
What was the service
he rendered?
How did he really
help us?
>   It was
>   because he wanted
>   to show us,
>   who we human beings
>   really *are,*
>   full of possibilities,
>   full of potentialities,
>   good and divine,
>   helpful and glorious,
>   loving and sustaining,
>   *full*
>   *of*
>   *the*
>   *glory*
>   *of*
>   *God,*

great and mighty,
open,
and relating to
all.
It was
because he wanted
to show us
that we aren't
nobodies,
but somebodies
full of spirit, life, and pep,
reflection
of God,
created in *their* image
free,
being able to break
through ourselves
caring for all.
    And one day
    there came to him
    those two sons of Zebedee,
    who only wanted
    to care for themselves,
    who wanted his glory
    for themselves
    alone.
Jesus did not refuse
their request;
he did not throw them
out;
he did not ridicule
their desire;
he only said,
if you want to be
all that you are,
don't think only
of yourself,
don't think only
of where to sit,

don't think only
of how to be served,
but do as I do,
break through yourself,
cross yourself out,
give yourself up,
in view of others
to serve them
and greater
you will never be able
to be,
you will be
with it
all.
    Aren't we all
    acting as
    daughters and sons,
    of that Zebedee?
Don't we all need
Jesus' answer
to be
all we are:
like him
daughters and sons
not of Zebedee,
but of
God?

52.

ON SEEING AND FOLLOWING

Mark 10:46–52

Bartimaeus was sitting
in the street
blind,
useless,
not counted,
nameless.
People never used his own name,
they only called him
"son of,"
the son of Timaeus.
He had given up,
he had been sitting there
for years,
with his cloak
as a tent
pulled around him,
shelter against the cold,
      against the sun,
      against the rain,
      against the dogs,
      against the crowd,

the only protection he had
for himself,
for his bag.
>He did not move,
>he moved as little as possible,
>he had learned that,
>too,
>only now and then
>his hand would appear
>from under the cloak,
>to receive
>a penny,
>or a nickel,
>or a piece of bread.
Suddenly
there was that noise,
at the entrance of the street.
It grew louder and louder,
it came nearer and nearer,
he quickly crept away
from his gutter in a corner,
pulling his cloak even tighter
around himself,
he had been before
in crowds.
It is no good
to be blind
in the excitement of a crowd.
>Then he heard the name of Jesus,
>and people singing,
>"Alleluia!"
>It was no riot,
>it was no lynching party,
>it was Jesus
>who passed.
>He opened his cloak
>and he shouted,
>but they told him
>to stop that,

but he shouted
even louder and louder:
"Son of David,
have pity on me!
Suddenly he felt
that all around him
things were changing.
He heard a voice
that called him forward,
he heard other voices
that told him to get up,
finally he understood,
he threw his cloak away,
came up,
and was guided to Jesus,
who said:
"What do you want me
to do for you?"
"Master,"
the nameless Bartimaeus
answered:
"Master,
I would like to see!"
And Jesus said:
"Be on your way!
Your faith
has healed you."
His faith had healed him,
his own faith,
did you hear that?
Did you really hear that?
This miracle
is that last one
told by the Gospels.
It is the last one,
because it is different.
After the other healings
the people healed go home,
to their families,

to their work,
to their jobs,
to their chores,
to their fields,
to their boats,
to their money
taking up their lives
again,
which had been interrupted
by their ailments.
    Bartimaeus
    did not do
    that.
    Bartimaeus
    never even looked back
    at his cloak,
    but he started to follow him
    from that day.
    Hadn't he told him:
    "Be on your way,"
    even before he saw?
His faith
had healed him,
his faith
would heal others,
he was going to do
the things Jesus did,
and even greater things
would he do,
following him,
as we should,
in our turn.
    So many of us
    seem to be nameless,
    too,
    being blind,
    being still blind.

53.

ON LISTENING AND LOVING

Mark 12:28–34

"Which is the supreme
commandment?"
they asked him,
and his answer
was:
"Hear!"
    He quoted
    the old Jewish prayer,
    Shema,
    each faithful Hebrew believer
    prayed every morning,
    "Hear,
    O Israel!"
Did you ever hear
of a deaf prophet?
I never did.
I've heard about blind ones,
and crippled ones,
but never about
a deaf one.
They all could hear,

they all did listen,
from Abram,
who answered:
    "I go!"
to Jonah,
who first said:
    "I don't go,"
but finally
went.
    Did you ever hear about
    a faithful believer
    who saw God?
    I never did,
    but I know of many
    who heard God,
    from Mary,
    who said:
        "Yes,
        here I am!"
    when she understood
    her mission,
    to her son Jesus himself
    who repeated,
    in the sweat and the tears,
    in the frustration and the anguish
    of the garden
    the answer
    he had learned from his mother:
        "Yes,
        here I am,
        your will
        be done!"
He had always
listened,
not only to that first word
"Hear!"
but to the rest
of the prayer,
too:

"The Lord, our God,
is Lord alone,
therefore you shall love
the Lord your God
with all your heart,
with all your soul,
with all your mind,
and with all your strength!"

It was because of that listening
that he had come into this world,
that he had left Nazareth,
and was on his way to Jerusalem.
It was because of that listening,
that he added
—in the name
of God—
"This first command
is equal to the second:
Love your neighbor
as yourself."

Loving God
we should make
God's love
our own,
as each lover
does
to the love
of the loved one.

We should love
our neighbors,
as God loves them,
as God loves us.
They should love
us,
as God loves us,
as God loves them.

It is that love
God is looking for,

it is that love
we are looking for,
it is that love
everyone is looking for.
     It is that love
     God is longing for
     and we are longing for,
     too,
     and nothing lives for us,
     except
     this long deep want,
     as everyone
     who is created
     in God's image
     feels from birth to death.
When someone would ask us,
what should I do
in view of you,
wouldn't our answer be:
     "Listen,
     listen to me!"
          The consequence
          of hearing this word
          was drawn by Jesus,
          it is not drawn
          by us.
We remain accomplices,
maintainers,
and perpetrators
of the injustices
in this world,
building
and keeping up
the structures and policies
that cause the death
and the misery
of millions
and billions,

—ourselves included—
as we do not listen,
and do not hear
the invitation
to God's love.
    It is that love
    that explains
    the vulnerability of God
    Emmanuel,
    Jesus,
    among us!
    God
    wants to be loved!
    Wasn't the supreme command
    God gave
    an invitation,
        "Hear,
        oh, listen,
        Israel.
        Love me!"

54.

ON GIVING ONESELF

Mark 12: 38–44

He came to the temple.
He walked a bit around,
and then sat down,
opposite the treasury,
near the offering blocks,
in which people
from all over the world,
dressed in all kinds of ways,
put their money,
their temple tax.
> He was just sitting there,
> while his disciples walked around,
> as we so often sit
> in a station or an airport,
> having nothing to do,
> so we watch.
We watch the people
who are passing by,
we see how they are hurrying,
we see how they walk,
we observe how they are dressed,

and we judge:
    "Good grief,
    look at the one there,
    in that red and that green,
    whoever dresses
    like that?"
He was watching them,
too,
judging and evaluating.
He saw
how the rich were coming
with bags full of money,
copper and silver,
and sometimes even golden coins.
    He saw
    how they were dressed
    flamboyantly,
    in silk and purple,
    in linen and brocade;
    he saw
    how they were surrounded
    by bodyguards,
    guardsmen and servants,
    temple police and priests,
    by porters and slaves,
    then,
    he saw
    her,
    with some difficulty
    remaining in line
    with all those
    important ones,
    heading
    for the offering box
    in her turn.
    She looked very poor,
    neatly,
    but shabbily dressed,

in the clothes of a widow,
within her closed hand
a piece of cloth.
When it was her turn,
she undid a knot
in that piece of cloth,
and while the others
were gesturing to her
to hurry,
and get it done with,
she produced
her two copper coins,
everything she had,
not even worth
a penny.
    He stood up,
    and called his followers together;
    he pointed to her,
    while she disappeared
    around the corner
    and said:
    "That widow there
    gave more
    than all the others,
    she gave all she had
    to live on,
    she gave herself."
I remember the story
I once heard
about a child
at Christmas,
under the Christmas tree.
She was sitting there alone,
she had asked for three presents,
she got more than ten,
she was sitting there
alone,
she was weeping,

because even that day,
her father and her mother
had not any time
to be with her;
she cried, and she yelled:
     "I don't want your gifts,
     please,
     I want you,
     be with me,
     today,
     on Christmas!"
She tried to phone,
but the phone
remained
dead.
     Did it never happen to you
     that you so dearly loved one,
     and he gave you the nicest of gifts,
     a diamond,
     worth even two months of his salary,
     and you said,
          "Oh, no,
          I don't want that,
          I want
          you!
          I am not interested
          in your gifts,
          I only want them
          insofar
          as they give you
          to me,
          please, please!"
According to Jesus,
God reacted like that,
watching those people,
emptying their large bags
full of gold and silver,
in honor of themselves,

giving from their surplus,
that was all they did.
God also reacted like that
when he saw
that poor widow,
who giving
all she had,
who giving
what she needed,
gave herself.
    That is what
    Jesus told them
    that day.
    Being loved and loving
    is the way God exists,
    just as
    we do.
    Amen.

55.

ABOUT THE END

Mark 13: 24–32

We are surrounded
by threatening signs.
There is no doubt
about that.

> Volcanoes are exploding,
> whole continents are shaking,
> there is famine and drought,
> new sicknesses appear,
> immune systems break down,
> there are wars all over,
> with bombs,
> with napalm,
> and with gas.

It is rather obvious
that something is going to happen.
The end seems near,
very near.

> Many are scared,
> many are panicking,
> many are losing their heads,

trying to protect themselves,
by building shelters,
by buying arms,
by organizing *star wars*,
by following very strict diets,
by exercising their bodies daily,
but everyone knows,
that in the final instance,
at the final trumpet blast,
none of this is going to help,
the end is near,
very near.
It is nearer
and nearer,
every single day.
And mind you,
don't think only
about the end of this world,
but think about
the end of you
in this world
independent of that final end.
What about your death?
That moment
no one will be able to avoid,
though it might sometimes
be delayed.
An end
has been near to us
before,
when were nicely
wrapped and packed
in the wombs of our mothers,
warm and humid,
comfortable and well protected,
growing rapidly,
provided with everything we needed,
cosily and lovingly.

Growing in that way,
we were at the same time
growing away,
growing out of that womb,
growing to the moment,
that that universe,
the first one we knew,
would be shattered
and shaken,
broken up
and upset,
growing to the moment
that we would be forced
through a very dark tunnel,
out of that womb
in a totally new life.
That passage
must have been very frightening.
It was so frightening
that none of us
spontaneously remembers it,
but we made it,
we went through it,
and at the end
of that tunnel,
we found the world
in which we live now.
At the end
of that tunnel
all those were waiting
who made our lives here possible,
parents and family,
friends and acquaintances,
and even
Jesus.
It is in that way
that we should understand
the Gospel of today.

Jesus tells us
that there will come an end
to the world
in which we live now.
That it should be seen
as another womb,
though it so very often
does not seem to be anything
but a deadly tomb.
> He tells us
> how to look at the signs,
> the dying sun and moon,
> the crumbling mountains,
> the drying up of water and rain,
> the wars and the sicknesses,
> we should struggle against
> night and day.
He warns us:
we will have to go
through a tunnel again,
the dark tunnel
of death.
> He warns us
> not to be like fools
> who put all their trust
> in this world,
> building houses
> and getting rich
> as if they would be here
> all the time.
Jesus does not say
all this to frighten
or to threaten us.
> Isn't he waiting
> at the other end
> of that tunnel
> together with all those we knew
> and who went before us,

just like that very first time,
they all will be there,
parents and our family
friends and acquaintances,
and even Jesus too.
Isn't he standing
at the other side
of the door?

56.

ROYAL PEOPLE

Mark 18:33–37

Kings do not exist anymore,
queens don't either.
The ones we still have
are only remnants from the past,
impositions,
antiquities,
well kept
but no longer functional.
    Kings and queens
    do still exist
    in the world of the fairy tales,
    where children,
    young ones and old ones,
    tell their stories
    of people
    who ruled in such a way
    that there was peace
    and prosperity,
    justice
    and equity,

and a prince for each princess
all over the land.
When people were in need,
when people were badly off,
when people were starving,
when people were frustrated,
when people were enslaved,
they always started to tell stories
of a king,
or of a queen,
who would rule
and reign
in such a way
that the seasons would follow each other
harmoniously,
that the sun would shine
during the day,
and the moon
during the night,
that the plants would grow,
and the herds increase,
that the fruits would swell,
that fish would be caught
in every crystal-clear water stream,
that everybody would be happy
and find a place,
a husband,
a wife,
with plenty of children,
in the world in which they lived,
everywhere.
    The Hebrews
    had that dream and desire so often
    during their history.
    When they were in difficulties
    they would pray:
        "Yahweh,
        give us a king!"

and when they had one
who was more part of the problem
than part of the solution,
they would pray again:
        "Yahweh,
        give us a king,
        a new one,
        a *real* one,
        the one we have
        is fake!"
That is why
they even tried to make
Jesus
their king.
But he had refused,
walking away from them.
        Now Pilate asked:
            "Are you king?
        His answer was:
            "Yes,
            I am a king,
            but not like the one
            you are thinking of.
            Subjects
            I have not
            in this world!
            Yes,
            a King,
            I am."
Hadn't he come in this world,
to fulfill that old dream,
hadn't he come in this world
to rid us of evil and sin,
hadn't he come into this world
to redeem and liberate us?
Hadn't he come into this world
to bring us justice and peace,
to ban wars and armies?

Wasn't that the reason
that God had sent him
into this world?
        "Yes,
        I am a King,
        but not like the one
        you are thinking of.
        Subjects
        I have not
        in this world!"
And then he starts to speak
about all those
who are listening to him,
who are hearing his voice,
who believe his truth.
        Is he suggesting
        that we
        are
        or should be
        queens and kings,
        too?
Queens and kings
in the way humanity
has always been dreaming
about kings and queens.
Those who establish
justice and peace,
prosperity and health
for all.
        I think
        that it is what
        he was thinking about,
        King,
        he was and is,
        but shouldn't we
        be kings and queens
        like him?
        Aren't we
        of his royal stock?

Are you willing to be
king
or queen
like him?
You should,
that is what it is
all about.

INDEX OF SCRIPTURAL TEXTS